THE ULTIMATE

Tailgater's™
BIG TEN HANDBOOK

STEPHEN LINN

theultimatetailgater.com

[interactive blvd]™

An Interactive Blvd Book
interactiveblvd.com

The Globe Pequot Press

GUILFORD, CONNECTICUT

To buy books in quantity for corporate use
or incentives, call **(800) 962–0973**
or e-mail **premiums@GlobePequot.com.**

Design by Karen Williams [Intudesign.net]

Photographs: Illinois: Heather Coit, Indiana: Dave Snodgress, Iowa: Hanna van Zutphen-Kann, Michigan: T.J.
Hamilton, Michigan State: Jon Brower, Minnesota: Ben Garvin, Northwestern: Jerry Lai, Ohio State: Laurel Wise,
Penn State: Bradley Harris, Purdue: Andrew Hancock, Wisconsin: Grace Flannery

Special thanks to Barb Rishaw, Steve Ney, Ed Rode, Shanon Davis, Karen Williams, and Scott Adams for all of their
help and support with this project.

Library of Congress Cataloging-in-Publication Data is available on file.

ISBN 978-0-7627-4498-5

Manufactured in the United States of America

First Edition/First Printing

TABLE OF CONTENTS

THE BIG TEN

This is the conference of some of college football's most storied teams, rivalries, and successes. It is also the conference that laid much of the groundwork for organized college football. It is home to three of the four largest football stadiums in America. It has some of the country's largest tailgate parties. And it is a conference that has 11 teams but calls itself the Big Ten.

Here's how it all happened.

In 1895 a group of seven Midwest university presidents got together at the Palmer House in Chicago to talk about organizing and regulating intercollegiate sports. One of those regulations was restricting eligibility to enrolled, full-time students who "were not delinquent in their studies." This was a departure from the status-quo where schools would place "ringers" and even professional players on their college teams, and it set the tone for more honest

BIG TEN HEISMAN TROPHY WINNERS	
1935	Jay Berwanger, Chicago*
1939	Nile Kinnick, Iowa
1940	Tom Harmon, Michigan
1941	Bruce Smith, Minnesota
1944	Les Horvath, Ohio State
1950	Vic Janowicz, Ohio State
1954	Alan Ameche, Wisconsin
1955	Howard Cassady, Ohio State
1973	John Cappelletti, Penn State
1974	Archie Griffin, Ohio State
1975	Archie Griffin, Ohio State
1991	Desmond Howard, Michigan
1995	Eddie George, Ohio State
1997	Charles Woodson, Michigan
1999	Ron Dayne, Wisconsin
2006	Troy Smith, Ohio State

* Chicago was a member of the Big Ten Football Conference from 1895–1945.

competition. (Incidentally, the Palmer House is still around; you can learn more about it in the Northwestern chapter on page 99.)

The following year the Big Ten—more formally known as the Intercollegiate Conference of Faculty Representatives—was formed with founding members Chicago, Illinois, Michigan, Minnesota, Northwestern, Purdue, and Wisconsin. Three years later, in 1899, Indiana and Iowa (now the University of Iowa) joined. Ohio State joined the conference in 1912. Michigan State College (now Michigan State University) was added to the ranks in 1949.

The only school to leave the Big Ten is the University of Chicago (although Michigan left in 1907 and rejoined in 1917). Just 4 years after the school's Jay Berwanger was awarded the first Heisman Trophy in 1935, the university's president abolished Chicago's football team, saying the school should focus on academics, not athletics. Chicago withdrew from the Big Ten in 1946 and focused on academics until 1969 when the school reintroduced football. Today the University of Chicago plays in Division III.

For 40 years the Big 10 had ten teams. But in 1993 Penn State joined the conference as the Big Ten's 11th team.

The Big Ten has some of the longest-running, most heated rivalries in the country. ESPN calls the annual Michigan–Ohio State match-up the greatest rivalry in all of sports. Every team in the conference is part of a traveling trophy rivalry. Among the best known is the Little Brown Jug that goes to the winner of the Michigan–Minnesota game (see page 83). Paul Bunyan has a part in two games: the Paul Bunyan Trophy (for the winner of the Michigan–Michigan State game) and Paul Bunyan's Axe (to the victor between Wisconsin and Minnesota).

Another trophy that has found its way to the Big Ten is the Heisman Trophy. Big Ten players have won it 16 times. And seven conference schools have brought home the national championship trophy—a few several times.

VENUE AND PRICING GUIDES

For each city in the Big Ten, I've included a campus snapshot that includes a tailgating venue guide. That's what all the icons are; use the chart below to learn what you can and can't do outside the stadium. At the time this book was printed all of the information was correct; but things can change, so be sure to check the school's Web site or call ahead if you have any questions.

For restaurants and attractions in the area, I've included a pricing guide to help you manage your budget. A quick note about the suggestions for things like restaurants and hotels: as a rule, I haven't included chains in the list. I figure you can find a Denny's or Hilton on your own. I've included suggestions for places unique to the city that you won't find anywhere else.

 Decorations are allowed, excluding banners and signs that are advertising services or goods.

 Alcohol is permitted for those of legal drinking age.

 Grills or cookers are permitted for noncommercial use only.

 Parking is more than $50 per day for cars or larger vehicles.

 Parking is between $30 and $50 per day for cars or larger vehicles.

 Parking is no more than $30 per day for any vehicle.

 RVs may park overnight before or after the game.

 Number of hours you can tailgate before game. Times exceeding 4 hours are included in "4" icon.

 Number of hours you may remain after the event. Usually this includes tailgating, but read the entry to be sure.

 RVs, limos, and other oversized vehicles are allowed.

 Tents may be erected.

 Tables, chairs, and other tailgating furniture are allowed.

 Venue offers visible security presence in parking and tailgating areas.

 Venue offers at least one paved parking lot.

 Shuttle service is available from parking or tailgating areas to the event and back again.

Pricing Guide for Restaurants and Attractions

Restaurants (based on average entrée price):

$	$1–$19
$$	$20–$39
$$$	$40+

Attractions (based on average general admission price):

$	$1–$9
$$	$10–$19
$$$	$20+

ILLINOIS

University of Illinois: 36,738 students
Urbana-Champaign, IL: pop. 67,518
Memorial Stadium: seats 69,249
Colors: Orange and Blue
Nickname: Fighting Illini
Mascot: None (Chief Illiniwek retired 2007)
Phone: (866) ILLINI-1

RVs and tailgaters arrive as early as 7 a.m. RVs park in Lot A, $35; cars are $15. Visitors should arrive at stadium from south or east for easier parking. No balloons or banners with ads; no open fires; no political campaigning. Tents must be 10 x 10 feet or smaller.

Shuttle Info: All parking within walking distance; no shuttles needed.

Fighting Illini Media Partners: 1400-AM WDWS, 97.5-FM WHMS

The University of Illinois is made up of three campuses, but the flagship is in Urbana-Champaign, which was founded as the Illinois Industrial University in 1867.

John Milton Gregory moved to Illinois to start the school—what he hoped would become the "West Point for the working world." He experimented with student government, instituted a liberal arts education, and battled criticism from legislators and others who wanted an industrial curriculum.

In the 1880s the school changed its name to the University of Illinois (this helped to eliminate confusion with schools for delinquents with similar names to the Illinois Industrial University), but then hit hard times financially. In the mid-1880s the university even tried to sell some of its land to make ends meet.

By the end of the century, the school had new administration, more stable finances, and fraternities. That last one was popular, and by 1920 Illinois was known across the country as one of the strongest fraternity campuses in America. Social life is still an important part of its campus life.

But it was the school's growing athletic life that caught the eye of Scott Williams. He had played football at State Normal University, so when he saw a notice for those interested in playing football at his new school, the University of Illinois, he was excited. At least until he got to the practice.

What he saw—students kicking and chasing a ball around a field—wasn't anything like football. So he gathered the group and taught them what they were supposed to do with the football, how to score, and some of the strategy of the game. He became the de facto coach.

The next year Williams went to university administrators with a deal: let his team represent Illinois in football, and the team would pay for its uniforms and expenses. They took the deal, and on October 2, 1890, Williams became coach, captain, and quarterback of the first University of Illinois football team. They took on Illinois Wesleyan and lost.

Illinois got a second chance in November and beat Wesleyan. The Illini ended its first season 1-2.

The next season, with new coach Robert Lackey, a better organized Illinois team went 6-0; it was the first of a series of winning seasons for the Illini. Included in those winning seasons were ones coached by Robert Zuppke who guided the team for 29 years, including 1914, 1919, 1923, and 1927. Those 4 years Illinois won the national championship.

While Williams is the guy credited with starting the football program, it's two other guys who are credited with putting the Illini on the map. You've probably heard of them: Red Grange and Dick Butkus. They are the only two Illinois players to have their numbers retired.

Grange (whose real first name was Harold) got his nickname "The Galloping Ghost" while at Illinois after a legendary performance against Michigan in 1924 (he played for Illinois from 1923 to 1925). There were several other legendary games, too, of course. When the Football Writers Association chose an All-American player to honor college football's 100th anniversary in 1969, the choice was unanimous: Red Grange. He was also in the charter class for both the College and Pro Football Halls of Fame.

Butkus, who played from 1962 to 1964, is the Illinois linebacker whose name adorns the trophy the NCAA awards to the outstanding college linebacker each year. He won his share of awards with other people's names on them, too, including the American Football Coaches Association Player of the Year in 1964 and the Walter Camp All-Century Team, and he came in third for the Heisman Trophy his senior year.

There are also some other football greats who spent time in Champaign-Urbana, among them George Halas and Ray Nitschke.

School Mascot

"Illinois" is how the French changed the spelling of Illiniwek (pronounced *ill-EYE-nih-wek*) when naming what became the state of Illinois. The Illiniwek

Confederation of Native Americans was a loose confederation of Algonquin tribes that lived in the region. The name translates to "the complete human being," and football coach Robert Zuppke (who coached from 1913 to 1941) felt that was an appropriate moniker for his team; he is credited with suggesting Chief Illiniwek become the school's mascot.

In 1926 the assistant band leader came up with the idea of having a student dressed as Chief Illiniwek perform an American Indian dance during Illinois's football halftimes. The costume was handmade, but the chief was a hit.

It wasn't until 1930 that Chief Illiniwek got his first authentic costume. That summer the student who was wearing the costume at the time, A. Webber Borchers, hitchhiked his way to the Pine Ridge reservation in South Dakota in search of real American Indian regalia. After explaining his purpose, some Sioux women made an authentic outfit for Borchers to wear that season.

Since then there have been several authentic outfits. The current one was purchased from Oglala Sioux Chief Frank Fools Crow (a nation not associated with the Illiniwek) in 1983 and is topped off with a headdress of turkey feathers rather than the traditional eagle feathers since eagles are a protected species.

While some Native Americans support the use of the Indian imagery as Illinois's mascot—as the Oglala Sioux do—the descendants of the Illiniwek don't.

The Peoria Tribe of Indians of Oklahoma is the closest descendant of the Illiniwek; the tribe was relocated there in the 19th century. While the tribe's view of Chief Illiniwek has changed over the years, now the tribe would like the chief retired, saying it doesn't represent the tribe or the culture. After all, the tribe says, the costume is Sioux. In 2000 one tribal chief put it bluntly: "I don't know what the origination was, or what the reason was for the university to create Chief Illiniwek. I don't think it was to honor us, because, hell, they ran our [butts] out of Illinois."

The NCAA included Illinois on its list of schools that use mascots with what it calls "hostile and abusive American-Indian nicknames," and banned the school (along with several other universities) from hosting postseason games until the nickname was discontinued. The University of Illinois appealed the ruling, pointing to comments from other Native Americans who have supported the Chief Illiniwek mascot, but the appeals failed. The NCAA did allow the school to continue using the Fighting Illini nickname, saying "Illini" referred to the state, not the tribe.

As I write this there hasn't been a decision on a mascot

Illinois Fight Song

"March of the Illini"

We are marching for dear old Illini
For the men who are fighting for you
Here's a cheer for our dear
Alma Mater
May our love for her ever be true
While we're marching along
life's pathway,
May the Spirit of old Illinois
Keep us marching and singing
In true Illini Spirit
For our dear old Illinois

successor to the chief, but Illini fans are weighing in with options at retirethechief.org/alternatives.html.

Since the name "Illini" gets to hang around, you may be wondering about its history. The earliest known use of the term at the university was in 1874 when the student newspaper changed its name from *The Student* to *The Illini.* According to an editorial in the paper they made up the name. The first time Illini was attached to an athletic team was in 1907 when it was applied to the football team, although the term didn't become popular until around 1915. The word *fighting* was added to the moniker when the fund-raising campaign to build Memorial Stadium used the phrase "Fighting Illini" in its efforts. That was in 1921.

Game-Day Traditions
Block-I

In 1910 a pep club formed to provide entertainment at various Illini athletic events, including football. They called themselves "Block-I," and although they weren't an official school group, by 1924 they had settled in as permanent residents for home football games in the east stands of Memorial Stadium. They did more than just cheer; they also performed card stunts during games to interact with fans and generate crowd enthusiasm (no, not the kind of card stunts Criss Angel does). For a couple of decades, a second batch of Block-I students set up shop in the west stands and mirrored what the kids in the east stands did.

In 2004 Block-I merged with I-Pride, the official support group of Illinois athletics. Well, the *Is* have it. This spirit group is now the largest student organization in the state with more than 2,700 spirited members. That's who's wearing all those orange shirts in the student section of Memorial Stadium and flipping the 8,000 cards during the game and halftime.

Visiting Illinois

The twin cities of Champaign and Urbana share the Illinois campus. Champaign was founded in 1855 and was called West Urbana since organizers built their town around railroad tracks laid just a couple miles west of Urbana, the county seat. It became Champaign in 1860. While the university is the center of attention here, the technology and software industries make up a good part of the area economy, along with a Kraft Foods plant. And if you're looking for some Urbana trivia, you're in luck: in the 1968 movie *2001: A Space Odyssey*, the famed computer HAL 9000 was programmed in Urbana.

Where to Stay

❶ Akademika: This B&B is located one block from campus. There are three guestrooms available, one of them a 700-square-foot suite comprising the entire top floor. The remaining rooms have shared baths. All rooms are nonsmoking and equipped with Internet-ready computers. The décor here is sparse and uncluttered, the antithesis of a Victorian B&B. Rooms run from $120 to $180

during big football weekends. (*(217) 344-2739, akademika.home.insightbb.com*)

❷ The Historic Lincoln Hotel: Built in 1924, this Tudor-style hotel is one of Urbana's more unique lodging options. You can choose between 128 suites, bi-level lofts, or rooms with king or queen beds—many have four posters and canopies. Floors have oriental carpets, and those canopies are all a rich red. There are other red touches, along with cream and gold. The overall feeling is sort of Old Bavaria meets Little House on the Prairie. During important game weekends rooms run $225–$432 and carry a two-night minimum. (*(217) 384-8800, historiclincolnhotel.com*) **❸ Lindley House:** Just four blocks from the university, this gingerbread Victorian home has four guestrooms and a carriage house for longer stays. Rooms are an eclectic mix of Victorian and other elements. The third-floor king suite has a private bath; guestrooms on the second floor share facilities. Rates run $95–$170 with a two-night minimum during football weekends. (*(217) 384-4800, lindley.cc*) **❹ Prairie Pines Campground:** About 15 miles north of the Illinois campus, this city park campground offers 95 sites with full hookups. Sites are large and level with gravel parking pads, surrounded by shade trees. Each site has a concrete patio and sidewalk to the street. Bathrooms and shower facilities are clean, as are the grounds. Site fees are $20 from April to October. Prices drop in November to $18; however, no water is available from November until spring. (*(217) 893-0438, village.rantoul.il.us/recreation/facilities/prairiepines/*) ❺ **Senator's Inn:** Located 5 minutes from campus, this three-story, brick Colonial has eight guestrooms, half with private baths. The large guestrooms strike a good balance between Victorian and modern aesthetics with wood floors, oriental rugs, and well-chosen furnishings and accents. The inn has an attached pub, with weekend entertainment. Rooms run $100–$200 during peak times, and may require a two-night minimum stay. (*(217)352-0002, senatorsinn.com*)

Where to Eat

TAILGATER SUPPLIES: ❶ **Common Grounds Food Co-op:** With very few exceptions, this Champaign co-op's produce is organic and, whenever possible, locally grown. Prices on most items are pretty competitive, too, which means everybody—the farmer, the store, and you—wins. Common Grounds sells lots of produce and food stuff, but doesn't sell meat or fish. (*(217) 352-3347, commonground.coop*) ❷ **The Market at the Square:** On average, 75 vendors set up shop each Saturday from May to November showcasing products

including meats, prepared foods, produce, kettle corn, herbs and sprouts, flowers, and plants. You'll also find home and garden furniture, handicrafts, jewelry, original artwork, clothing, soaps and lotions, and much more. It's not just a market, it's a community event. (*(217) 384-2319, ci.urbana.il.us, click on "Quick Link" then scroll to "Market at the Square" link*)

SPORTS BARS: ❸ **Billy Barooz Pub & Grill:** Inside it's very bright with lots of windows. Large, plasma TVs cover practically every inch of the building. The bar area, which is dominated by pub tables, is decorated with banners of Big Ten universities. The grill area, which has booths and tables, has photos of old-time downtown Champaign on the walls. (*$, (217) 355-8030*) ❹ **Illini Inn:** Home of the Mug Club, and a great dive bar, with carved etchings all over the wooden walls, tables, and chairs. (*$, (217) 344-5209*)

RESTAURANTS: ❺ **Bacaro Wine Bar & Italian Restaurant:** This award-winning restaurant attracts a sophisticated crowd with its Euro-chic atmosphere. Its menu of seasonal Italian fare probably draws them in, too, with dishes like flatiron steak rubbed with smoked paprika. Bacaro's decor is simple, airy, and clean, allowing the food to remain center stage. Their 180-plus Italian wines are half-price on Sundays. (*$$, (217) 398-6982, bacaro.thadmorrow.com*) ❻ **Kamakura:** This Champaign sushi and teppanyaki restaurant lets you feel like Japan's green rice paddies are waiting outside. Rice paper "shoji" screens soften the dining room. Kamakura stresses handmade and homemade food, and all sauces and dressings are the owner's original creations, made in-house daily. *Gyoza*, the steamed Chinese dumplings popular in Japan, are hand-wrapped every morning too. (*$–$$, (217) 351-4332, kamakurasteakhouse.com*)

❼ **Silvercreek:** Housed in a restored lumber mill, the interior includes dark trim, brick walls, and a vaulted ceiling with exposed beams. There's also a large greenhouse dining area. Silvercreek serves straight-ahead American cuisine. The salmon is wild, the beef and chicken are both free-range, and the duck is antibiotic, steroid, and hormone free (as are the other meats). They also offer some outstanding vegetarian entrées. Locals warn you to save room for John's Chocolate Solution cake, with a bittersweet chocolate mousse. (*$$, (217) 328-3402, couriersilvercreek.com*)

Daytime Fun

❶ **Chanute Air Museum:** From barnstormers to bombers, this is the largest aerospace museum in Illinois. Just north of Champaign, the museum has exhibits about the history of aviation in Illinois and the accomplishments of the air field and Chanute Air Force Base. You can also learn about engineer and aviator Octave Chanute who wrote *Progress in Flying Machines* in 1894 and was a mentor to the Wright Brothers. (*$, (217) 892-5774, aeromuseum.org*) ❷ **Curtis Orchard & Pumpkin Patch:** Pick your own apples from their 4,500-tree orchard, or grab

something from the 20-acre pumpkin patch to take home. This 80-acre farm also has an outdoor maze, play area, and petting zoo for children, along with a bakery and café (locals say have a doughnut). For a small fee you can take in a farm wagon ride on weekends and live entertainment on Sundays. (*Free–$, (217) 359-5565, curtisorchard.com*)   ❸ **Krannert Art Museum:** The museum's permanent collection of 9,000 objects includes pieces of Asian, African, European, and American art. In addition, the museum—which is located on campus—hosts several rotating exhibitions each year. (*Free, (217) 244-0516, kam.uiuc.edu*) ❹ **Orpheum Children's Museum:** The New Orpheum Theatre opened in 1914 as a vaudeville and movie theater. Well, it isn't new anymore, and it isn't a theatre anymore: it's a children's museum. Several interactive exhibits engage children to learn about science, health, art, and more. The Design-a-Dinosaur exhibit lets you mix-and-match dinosaur parts to create your own. A bit of trivia: The building is a one-third scale replica of the opera hall at Versailles. (*$, (217) 352-5895, m-crossroads.org/orpheum/index.html*)

Nighttime Fun

❶ **Canopy Club:** This is the Urbana destination for live music and a rainforest theme. Really. The Canopy in the name is a reference to the "roof" of the rainforest, and the bar is decorated in the same vein. Bands as diverse as Maroon 5 and Bela Fleck, along with local and regional acts, have the place packed on weekends. Basic bar menu with one exception: the meat products are veggie substitutes. The Canopy also promotes environmental and related causes. (*$–$$, (217) 367-3140, jaytv.com/can2*) ❷ **The Highdive:** This hip dance club downtown books diverse bands like Black Eyed Peas, Buckwheat Zydeco, and The White Stripes, as well as popular local and regional acts. When live acts aren't on-stage, a DJ keeps things moving. The bar has a wide variety of beers; the kitchen has only finger foods. But no one comes here to eat, anyway. (*$–$$, (217) 356-2337, thehighdive.com*) ❸ **Joe's Brewery:** This restaurant/bar/beer garden/dance club is a favorite of Illinois students and locals. Live bands play in the beer garden; DJs are in charge of music inside on the dance floor. There are also TVs to watch a game, darts, and more. The menu

includes the basics—burgers and pizzas are popular. It's also the place to see and be seen Fridays and Saturdays, so get here early. (*$, (217) 384-1790, joesbrewery.com*) ❹ **Soma Ultralounge:** It's hip. It's urban. It's sleek. Soma is a dance bar with a long list of cocktails and beers, and a hip crowd that comes by for everything from Salsa & Meringue to hip-hop to R&B. Soma also hosts parties and special events. Their slogan is "anything can happen here, and does." You've been warned. (*$, (217) 359-7662, somaultralounge.com*)

Shopping

❶ **Downtown Champaign:** From vintage clothing to art, gifts to percussion instruments (in case you need a drum for game day), you'll find shops up and down the streets of downtown Champaign. It's a pleasant downtown area with several restaurants and bars for food and diversion too. (*downtown champaign.com*) ❷ **T.I.S College Bookstore:** This is Illini gear central. If you need something with the Illinois logo on it, you'll find it here. Besides the usual apparel and gifts, you'll find Chief Illniwek statuettes (at least they had them when I wrote this, but get them fast—once they're gone the only place you'll find them is eBay). You can also get tailgating supplies and car accessories to make sure your parking space is decked out in orange and blue. (*(217) 337-4900, tisbookui.com*)

INDIANA

Indiana University: 38,903 students
Bloomington, IN: pop. 69,291
Memorial Stadium: seats 52,354
Colors: Cream and Crimson
Nickname: Hoosiers
Mascot: None
Phone: (812) 855-0847

RVs arrive 6 p.m. Friday, park at Gate 11 for $40. Tailgating starts 7 a.m. Saturday. No tailgating during game, but tailgating may resume after game's end (enforced by university police). Lawn furniture's permitted, but not "indoor" furniture. Canopies are allowed but mustn't impede traffic. No tents or glass containers allowed. Overnight tailgaters should leave Sunday morning.

Shuttle Info: All parking within easy walking distance; no shuttles needed.

Hoosiers Media Partner: 105.1-FM WHCC

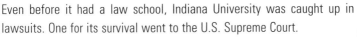

Even before it had a law school, Indiana University was caught up in lawsuits. One for its survival went to the U.S. Supreme Court.

It all started in 1824 when State Seminary opened as the state's first public university, fulfilling the Indiana legislature's requirement to create a state university with free tuition (that part's changed). The problem was there was already a Territory of Indiana public university (the school is now Vincennes University), and some thought it should be adopted as the state's public university, rather than building a new one. In 1853 Vincennes filed suit and the appeals went to the High Court. Of course, Indiana University won (by now State Seminary had been renamed Indiana University).

In 1867 IU made additional headlines, this time with the historic enrollment of Sarah Parke Morrison. Morrison was the school's first female student, and Indiana was one of the first state universities in America to

admit women on an equal basis with men. In 1873 Morrison accomplished another first: she became the first female professor at IU.

Another headline came in 1883, but this wasn't a good one. The school's original campus in Seminary Square burned to the ground. After previous fires the school had been rebuilt on the same land in the center of Bloomington, but this time the university rebuilt on the city's eastern edge. The first cornerstone was laid in 1894, and in 1908 the new campus was completed. The city has grown a great deal since then, of course, and today the campus is once again in the center of Bloomington.

Indiana's football team hasn't had too many headlines—at least not in national papers. The Hoosiers first took the field in 1884 and began regular play 3 years later. IU has never developed into a football powerhouse, having won just two conference championships (1945 and 1967) and earning trips to postseason bowls just a handful of times. In fact, the last coach to have a winning record at IU was Bo McMillin who coached in Bloomington from 1934 to 1947, leading the Hoosiers to an undefeated season and Big Ten championship in 1945.

One Hoosier has been inducted to both the College and Pro Football Halls of Fame. Pete Pihos was an All-American at IU playing in 1942–1943 and 1945–1946. He went on to play for the Philadelphia Eagles.

School Mascot

You know Indiana is the Hoosier State. You know IU is the Hoosiers. But what is a Hoosier, and how did it get tied to Indiana? That last one is a little more confusing.

The most popular explanation is that it is an alteration of an English word (as in the country) *hoozer,* which was used to describe anything really, really large. A dinosaur, for example, would be a *hoozer,* and Indianan, well . . . no one is sure how it got from one definition to the other.

The first definition of Hoosier in this country is from the 1820s when it meant "a big, burly, uncouth specimen of individual; a frontiersman, countryman, rustic," according to the *Dictionary of Americanisms.* It was one of several less-than-complimentary nicknames for citizens of a number of states at the time. Oklahomans were Okies (still are). Missourians were Pukes (but no more).

Another theory is the name came from military origins, but still is a mispronunciation of another word—in this case the European *huzar* or *hussar,* which meant something akin to "light horseman"
toward the end of the 15th century. This term, the explanation goes, was used to describe light cavalry regiments that fought in the Revolutionary War alongside George Washington. Later, during the Civil War, the Indiana regiment named their camp "Hoosiertown."

Either way, the name is now carried with pride by Indianans and the university, although there is no Hoosier running up and down the sideline on game day. Part of the reason for that is no one has been able to settle on what to use as a mascot to embody a Hoosier. But they've tried.

In 1935 the school had a white collie mascot. In 1952 it was The Hoosier Schoolmaster. The 1960s brought a bison and a bulldog. In 1979 IU debuted Hoosier Pride, a hillbilly—you can guess how that went over. It was gone inside a year.

In the 1980s the school used the tried-and-true contest to find a mascot. Finalists included a dragon, a gargoyle, and an illustration of a mascot called Henry Hoosier. School administrators didn't like what they saw and none was chosen.

Game-Day Traditions
Defend the Rock

The big limestone boulder in the north end zone of Memorial Stadium is "The Rock." That's also what they call the stadium now, and "Defend the Rock" is the Hoosier battle cry.

It started in 2005 when head football coach Terry Hoeppner nicknamed the stadium "The Rock." At the time the boulder was a fixture of the Mellencamp practice field, but the coach had it removed, put on a granite slab, and placed inside the stadium. A tradition was born and today players touch The Rock as they take the field to defend it.

And to answer your question, yes, Mellencamp practice field is named for *that* Mellencamp . . . it's John Cougar Mellencamp practice field.

The Walk

It's a newer tradition at IU, but Hoosier fans line up to cheer the team on its way to Memorial Stadium. The Walk at Indiana begins with the team buses driving around the perimeter of the parking area to make sure tailgating fans know the team has arrived. The players get off the buses along Woodlawn Avenue and begin their march toward Memorial Stadium. Tradition calls for the band to play

"Indiana," "Our Indiana," "Indiana Fight," and "R-O-C-K in the USA" for the fans lining the walkway before the team enters the gates of "The Rock."

"Indiana Fight"

In addition to "Indiana, Our Indiana," Hoosier fans also sing a more recent fight song—well, at least part of it. The entire song is rarely sung at games; the crowd usually sings only the words: "GO! IU! FIGHT! FIGHT! FIGHT! Indiana, we're all for you!"

But, in case you would like to sing it from beginning to end, here are the lyrics for "Indiana Fight":

Fight for the Cream and Crimson,
Loyal sons of our old IU
Fight for your Alma Mater,
And the school you love so true.
Fight for old Indiana,
See her victories safely through,
GO! IU! FIGHT! FIGHT! FIGHT!
For the glory of old IU.

Visiting Indiana

About an hour southwest of Indianapolis, Bloomington is best known as home to the University of Indiana and to the Kinsey Institute for Research in Sex, Gender, and Reproduction. The IU campus is considered one of the most

Illinois Fight Song

"Indiana, Our Indiana"

Indiana, Our Indiana
Indiana, we're all for you
We will fight for
The Cream & Crimson,
For the glory of Old IU
Never daunted, we cannot falter
In a battle, we're tried and true
Indiana, Our Indiana
Indiana, we're all for you!

beautiful in the nation—named in the top five by landscape artist Thomas Gaines in his book *The Campus as a Work of Art*. It is also home to the annual IU bicycle race the Little 500, which was featured in the Oscar-winning movie *Breaking Away*.

Where to Stay

❶ **Biddle Hotel & Conference Center:** This hotel and conference center (also called the Indiana Memorial Union Hotel) sits right on campus and is part of IU's big, rambling Student Union building, featuring a three-story bookstore, bowling alley, bakery, beauty shop, pool hall, and video game area, and several restaurants ranging from cheap to pricey. To get more of the campus life, you'll need to register for classes. Rooms run $73–$243, but during football season demand is so high reservations are made through a drawing. Get your name in by July 1, or you'll miss out. (*(800) 209-8145, imu.indiana.edu/hotel/index.shtml*)

❷ **Cedar Ridge Camping Resort:** This park opened in May 2005, so everything is rather new and clean here. There are 120 sites with full hookups. You won't get cable TV, phone, or modem hookups, but you will get very large pull-through and back-in sites. Regular sites run $32; concrete VIP sites are $40. If you don't use the sewer hookup, you won't be charged for it, making the price $26. *((800) 641-9308, campcedarridge.com)* ❸ **Century Suites:** This all-suite hotel offers 21 one- and two-bedroom suites, tricked out with fireplaces and whirlpool tubs. Suites are constructed like little Victorian townhouses, making the property resemble an English hamlet. Each suite has a well-equipped kitchenette, wireless Internet access, and a queen-size sleeper sofa in the living room. Suites run $155–$235 during football weekends, with a two-night minimum stay. They sell out months in advance, so call early. *((800) 766-5446, centurysuites.com)*

❹ **Fourwinds Resort & Marina:** It's a tropical-themed hotel on the banks of Lake Monroe, 15 minutes outside of town. Fourwinds's beautifully landscaped grounds are an outstanding plus, and the Polynesian theme actually looks pretty cute. Rooms are equipped with standard amenities, and are furnished in traditional (non-Polynesian) style. The hotel is undergoing a slow renovation; every winter, about 20 or more guestrooms receive updated furnishings and improved bathrooms. Rooms are $160 during football weekends. *((800) 824-2628, fourwindsresort.com)* ❺ **Grant Street Inn:** The inn offers 24 rooms, each individually decorated with antiques and other elegant furnishings. All rooms have private baths, color TVs, and phones. Many also offer fireplaces and separate entrances. Suites have whirlpool tubs. It's a B&B, so you get a hot

breakfast every day, too. Rooms run from $209 to $249. (*(812) 334-2353, grantsinn.com*) ❻ **Scholar's Inn:** It's a restored 115-year-old mansion, with 6 suites, all with private baths, telephones, and TV, with a complementary video library. Some rooms have a fireplace, Jacuzzi tub, fountain, or private patio. Rooms are individually decorated, and you can get a full breakfast served to you in bed each morning. Rooms at this B&B run $130–$150 during most football weekends, and may require a two-night stay. You can also grab a meal at **Scholars Inn Restaurant**, just a few steps away from the inn. (*(812) 332-1892, scholarsinn.com*) ❼ **Wampler House:** This B&B is nestled in the little village of Clear Creek, about 10 minutes from the IU campus. Built in 1857, the inn had a new, rather modern addition built on in 2003. Guests can choose between six rooms and two suites. All rooms have pillow-top mattresses, gas-log fireplaces, cable TVs/VCRs, telephones, and private baths with showers. During football weekends, rooms run $120–$210. (*(877) 407-0969, wamplerhouse.com*)

Where to Eat

TAILGATING SUPPLIES: ❶ **Bloomingfoods Market & Deli:** This supermarket co-op has two locations—the main East Store, and the smaller Downtown Store—and a café. Like most co-ops, Bloomingfood's emphasis is on wholesome, organic, sustainably grown foods, usually grown locally. You'll find all the produce, dairy, meats, and packaged foods you'd ever want here. Think of it as a farmers' market with indoor plumbing and climate control. (*(812) 336-5400 – East Store, bloomingfoods.org*) ❷ **Goods for Cooks:** Located in the downtown Bloomington square, this is a great place for tailgaters to pick up top-quality cooking tools and utensils, as well as gourmet sauces, spices, and seasonings. They also stock some great barbecue and grilling tools in case you left yours at home—or just want new ones. (*(812) 339-2200, goodsforcooks.com*)

SPORTS BARS: ❸ **Coaches Bar & Grill:** With 28 plasma screens, and memorabilia from nearly every IU coach dating back to 1887, this place is worth visiting. Also displayed are mementos of their selection of the 20 greatest coaches, including Bobby Knight and Larry Bird. It's a bit like a museum but without the theme-park cheesiness. The menu is a selection of wraps, sandwiches, and entrées, with better than average pub-grub appetizers. Coaches has 12 beers on tap and drink specials for every day of the week. (*$–$$, (812) 339-3537, coachesiu.com*) ❹ **Kilroy's Sports Bar:** It's one of the most popular sports bars in town. There are more than 30 TVs, including 2 150-inch

HDTVs and 8 big-screen TVs, so it's not like you won't see the game. The bar has two levels, with video games, pool tables, live entertainment, and enough outside seating to fit 400 IU fans on game day. (*$, (812) 333-6006, kilroys-bloomington.com*) ❺ **Yogi's Grill & Bar:** They've got more than 30 TVs, 5 of them big-screen HDTVs, within eye-shot of most anywhere in the bar. Yogi's also offers 40 beers on draft and a menu filled with sandwiches, salads, appetizers, and entrées. Locals recommend the nachos and pulled pork BBQ. If you've had enough football, hang out in Yogi's billiard room for a change of pace. (*$, (812) 323-9644, yogis.com*)

RESTAURANTS: ❻ **Café Django:** Named after French jazz legend Django Reinhardt, this intimate restaurant serves a diverse menu, with dishes from throughout Asia and other parts of the world. It's a cozy place, great for a date, or just relaxing with friends. There's live jazz on Friday and Saturday. Try the shumai or the momo. (*$, (812) 335-1297*) ❼ **Mother Bear's:** *People* magazine calls it one of the best pizza places in the United States. Mother Bear's has a full selection of classic pizza ingredients, plus a menu of creative gourmet pizzas that'll have you licking your lips. Mother's also serves some basic pasta dishes, hot subs, salads, and appetizers, but it's the pizza (and the stromboli sub) that's the star here. (*$, (812) 332-4495, motherbearspizza.com*) ❽ Janko's—Little Zagreb: This place serves the best steak in town, some say in the state. John Mellencamp, Bobby Knight, and Billy Joel have all eaten here (but I'm pretty certain not together). Aside from huge steaks, the menu also offers chicken, pork, and lobster, plus some very interesting Yugoslavian dishes. Surprisingly, the atmosphere's more like a diner than a steakhouse, with vinyl table cloths and very casual dress. (*$$, (812) 332-0694, littlezagreb.com*)

Daytime Fun

❶ Elizabeth Sage Historic Costume Collection: The Sage Collection at IU has more than 19,000 items showcasing men's, women's, and children's fashion and accessories of the past hundred years or so. Fashion dos and don'ts are on display. You'll need to call to find out where to see them since they don't have a permanent gallery space and hold their exhibitions around campus and the community. (*Free, (812) 855-5497, indiana.edu/%7Eamid/sage/sage.html*) ❷ Indiana University Art Museum: It started as a small university teaching collection in 1941, but today it is one of the best regarded university museums in

the country. You walk through architect I. M. Pei's triangular atrium to see more than 30,000 works ranging from ancient artifacts and African masks to paintings by Monet and Picasso to contemporary American art. The museum also hosts regular touring exhibits. (*Free, (812) 855-5445, iub.edu/~iuam/iuam_home.php*) ❸ **The Kinsey Institute:** Dr. Alfred C. Kinsey came to IU when the Association of Women Students convinced the school to create a course for students who were married or contemplating marriage. Kinsey was a Harvard-trained zoology professor and couldn't find much research to teach the course. So he created his own. The Kinsey Institute has become the world's most popular—and sometimes controversial—center for research in sex, gender, and reproduction. It has a huge collection of research, films, and videos, photographs, art, and artifacts pertaining to human sexuality. The Institute's gallery is open weekdays but only from 2:00 to 4:00 p.m., although you can call to arrange other tours. (*Free, (812) 855-7686, kinseyinstitute.org*) ❹ **Oliver Winery:** This is Indiana's oldest and largest winery and it all started as a hobby for an IU law professor. When William Oliver moved to Bloomington in 1959, he took up an interest in wine and started making it in his basement. In the 1970s he bought some land and planted more than 30 acres of vineyards. That's when it got serious. By the 1980s Oliver was buying grapes from outside the state and production was growing. In 2007 Oliver Winery, now run by the professor's son, is producing more than 500,000 gallons of wine. You can taste it (and buy it) during your tour of the vineyard. (*Free, (800) 25-TASTE,* oliverwinery.com) **❺ Tibetan Cultural Center:** Established in 1979 by the eldest brother of the Dalai Lama, who worked at IU, the Center includes a temple, cultural building, and 11 Mongolian gers, among other buildings. The center's mission is to help preserve Buddhist culture and tradition, and foster a cultural exchange program with Tibetans in Eastern Tibet. Visitors can take guided tours of the 108-acre center. Tours are free, but they ask for a "modest fee" for large groups. (*Free, (812) 331-0014, tibetancc.com*)

Nighttime Fun

❶ Nick's English Hut: It's been an IU student hangout for nearly 80 years, and probably will be for 80 more. This is a big place, too, with four bars and enough room to seat more than 500 people. I could have put Nick's in the sports bar category (after all, fans pile in to watch games on the bar's 30-plus TVs), but what folks come here for is to hang out and visit over a beer and a burger. They also serve other stuff like steaks and jambalaya. (Do they eat jambalaya in England?) (*$, (812) 332-4040, nicksenglishhut.com*)

❷ Tutto Bène Wine Café & More: The wine is the star here, but the tapas are worth coming for, too. The two go well together—as they have in Spain for centuries—since the appetizer-sized tapas are perfect to share around the table while you sample the extensive wine list. If you're wondering about the other parts of the name, "Tutto Bène" means "everything's good" and "& More" means they sell gift baskets, furniture, and art too. (*$, (812) 330-1060,*

bloomingtonwinecafe.com) ❸ **Uncle Fester's House of Blooze and Fester's Jungle Room:** First of all, you gotta love the names. Folks around the IU area like these sister establishments for a number of other reasons. They like the House of Blooze for the live music, dance tunes spun by DJs, and the drink specials. They like The Jungle Room for its big screen TV (they claim it's the biggest in the city), its collection of arcade games, and a menu that goes to extremes—from steaks to vegan dishes. (*$, (812) 323-1023, festered.net and festered.net/jr*)

Shopping

❶ **Bloomington Antique Mall:** For nearly 20 years this collection of booths (more than 120 of them) has housed southern Indiana's largest collection of antiques. Browsing the aisles you'll find Victorian furniture, china, silver, collectables, tools, and more. The mall's building is also an antique. Built in 1895, it was a wholesale food warehouse before being renovated to house the antique mall. (*(812) 332-2290, bloomingtonantiquemall.com*) ❷ **Downtown Bloomington:** Anchored by its historic courthouse, downtown Bloomington's tree-lined streets include a number of shops and galleries, as well as restaurants and night spots. Some unique stops include **Fossil Rain** for its fossil, mineral, and gemstone handcrafted jewelry, **Banana Junction** for its toys and gifts, and **Goods for Cooks** has tips and tools to kick your tailgate menu up a notch or two. (*downtownbloomington.com*) ❸ **Indiana Varsity Shop:** From infant onesies to replica jerseys with custom numbers and names, here you can outfit your Hoosier from crib to college and beyond. You can also get a tailgater hitch cover with a built-in bottle opener emblazoned with the IU logo. The Varsity Shop is part of the IU Bookstore on Seventh Street. (*(812) 855-4352, iuvshop.com*)

IOWA

University of Iowa: 26,000 students
Iowa City, IA: pop. 65,220
Kinnick Stadium: seats 70,397
Colors: Black and Old Gold
Nickname: Hawkeyes
Mascot: Herky
Phone: (319) 335-9431

RVs arrive 6 p.m. Friday, park in Lots 43, 1F, and 2F for $20 per day; cars pay $10. Free parking, shuttle service available from Hancher Commuter Lot and Hawkeye Commuter Lot, 2 hours prior to kickoff. Public parking for RVs available at Finkbine Golf Course and commuter lots. Tailgating may continue during game—just keep it within your space; leave glass containers home.

Shuttle Info: Hawkeye Express Train transports fans 3 hours prior to kickoff, resuming at start of fourth quarter. To ride, park south of U.S. Highway 6, south of Coral Ridge Mall. Round trip $10 per person, children 12 and under free. Lots O and P have free shuttle service.

Hawkeyes Media Partner: 800-AM KXIC

On December 28, 1846, Iowa became a state. Fifty-nine days later the state founded the State University of Iowa (the "State" was later dropped), although it wasn't until March 1855 that the school actually opened to students and became the first public university to admit men and women on an equal basis.

At the time Iowa City was the state capital and the university's original campus was the capitol building and 10 acres of land around it. Students didn't get to use what's now called the "Old Capitol" since the territorial government was using it. But in 1857 students got the run of the place when the state capital moved to Des Moines.

From 1857 to 1863 the Old Capitol housed the entire university including class-rooms, administrative offices, even a fire station. But the 1860s were hard on the school. Finances were tight (they cut the Old Capitol lawn and sold it for hay to make extra money), and the Civil War added additional hardships. Many classes were cancelled during the war, although the university was able to remain open. Students in the Military Department trained on campus using real weapons.

After the war, at the turn of the century, the school began work on buildings at each of the Old Capitol's four corners. The first was completed in 1902, the last in 1924, and the five buildings are now known as the Pentacrest and sit at the heart of campus. Along with the buildings, Iowa has grown its programs to become a national leader in health care—its hospitals and clinics have been ranked in "America's Best Hospitals" since the rankings began—and creative arts, as home to famed Iowa Writers' Workshop. The creative arts have a rich history at Iowa; it was the first university on the planet to place creative work in theater, writing, music, and art on an equal basis with academic research.

And if you have to go to the dentist while you're here, don't say anything bad about the Hawkeyes. Seventy-eight percent of the dentists in the state are Iowa grads.

It was after the Civil War, as the university began to regroup and rebuild, that football was introduced to the Iowa campus. It was a club sport when students began playing in 1872, but in 1889 the university fielded its first varsity football team and promptly lost its first game 24–0 to Grinnell. The next year they played Grinnell again, but this time at home on Iowa Field. It didn't matter; Iowa lost 14–6.

The team's third game was against Iowa Wesleyan College and the 91–0 victory helped everyone forget those two earlier losses.

Iowa had some tough years in the beginning, but by the turn of the century the Hawkeyes were beginning to dominate their opponents. From 1898 to 1901 Iowa won 23 straight games without allowing a touchdown. By 1913 Iowa was leading the nation in scoring (averaging more than 44 points a game), and the following year the team beat Northern Iowa by a margin that is still the largest in school history, 95–0. The 1921 Iowa team won the national championship.

But by the 1930s fortunes had changed at Iowa. The Depression hit the state and the school hard. Money was hard to come by. So were football wins. But in 1939 the Ironmen gave the state and Hawkeye fans something to cheer about.

The "Ironmen" nickname comes from Coach Eddie Anderson's speech to his team that unless the starters played the entire 60 minutes of each game, Iowa didn't have the depth to win. The starters came through and posted a 6-1-1 record and finished ninth in the nation. The star of the team was Nile Kinnick who played

halfback (although he might as well have been the quarterback since he led the team in passing), defensive back, punter, kicker, and special teams returner. His efforts won him the 1939 Heisman Trophy, and it's his name that adorns Iowa's football stadium today.

Of course the other name that is forever associated with Iowa football is Hayden Fry. He came to Iowa City in 1979 to take over a team that hadn't had a winning season in nearly 20 years. It took Fry a couple of seasons to turn that around, but by 1981 the Hawkeyes were 8-3, Big Ten champions, and playing in the Rose Bowl (although they lost to Washington 28–0). Fry's 1985 team was ranked #1 for 5 weeks, finished 10-1, and won Iowa's first outright Big Ten championship since 1958.

After 20 years, and a 143-89-6 record, Fry retired from Iowa and from football in 1998. Fry rebuilt Iowa into a winning program again and many of his assistants have become successful head coaches elsewhere. One of them has done that in Iowa City. Hawkeyes head coach Kirk Ferentz was Fry's offensive line coach from 1981 to 1989.

School Mascot

The pen of James Fenimore Cooper was the first to write the term *Hawkeye*. It's from his 1826 novel *Last of the Mohicans*. About a decade later, it became the

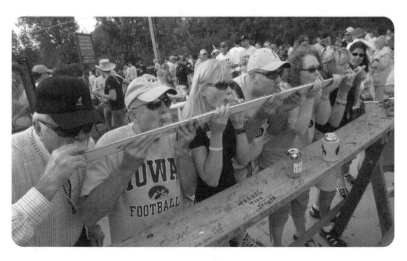

nickname for those living in the state of Iowa, and the school borrowed the state nickname as its own.

But what does a Hawkeye look like? That task was put to Dick Spencer who taught journalism at the university, as well as the only university-level editorial cartooning class in America.

Spencer took a trip to the school's Museum of Natural History to see if nature could spark an idea. He spent a lot of time looking at hawks and drew some lifelike sketches of one as a mascot idea. Then, just for fun, he sketched a smiling bird, waving a wing and wearing an Iowa sweater. It was this "cross between Woody Woodpecker and a bald eagle,"

Iowa Fight Song

The word is "Fight! Fight! Fight! for IOWA,"

Let every loyal Iowan sing;

The word is "Fight! Fight! Fight! for IOWA,"

Until the walls and rafters ring
(Rah! Rah!)

Come on and cheer, cheer, cheer, for IOWA

Come on and cheer until you hear the final gun.

The word is "Fight! Fight! Fight! for IOWA,"

Until the game is won.

as a university article put it, that caught the eye and enthusiasm of faculty and students and became the mascot.

Spencer gave it a look, but not a name. That came from John Franklin whose suggestion of Herky the Hawk won a state-wide contest.

Herky found his way to Korea during the Korean War as the insignia of the 124th Fighting Squadron and later, in the mid-1950s, found his way to the Iowa sidelines as a costumed mascot at football games.

Game-Day Traditions
Pink Locker Rooms

Okay, you're not going to see this Iowa tradition unless you're playing the Hawkeyes—literally. But it may have an effect on the outcome of the game.

Famed Iowa coach Hayden Fry (1979–1998) majored in psychology when he was at Baylor University. He may have traded in the couch for the shoulder pads, but his interest in how the mind works never went away.

One psychological theory he remembered from his studies was the effect of color on behavior. Pink, the theory goes, suppresses aggressive and hostile behavior, encouraging a calmer attitude. So Fry had the visitor's locker rooms painted and decorated in pink. Even the lockers themselves and the urinals are pink. It may have worked: Fry retired from Iowa with a record of 143-89-6 and three Big Ten titles.

The pink locker rooms remained after Fry's tenure but faced protests in 2005 from faculty and students who said they were demeaning to women and homosexuals. They demanded the pink be replaced. The protest failed and visiting players still use pink lockers and urinals at Kinnick Stadium.

Hawkeye Victory Polka

No, it's not a "Weird Al" Yankovic tune. It's the Hawkeye Marching Band's version of "In Heaven There Is No Beer," which it plays after Hawkeye victories. The band used to play it more often—like several times each game—but in 2001 the university president banned the song after critics said it was inappropriate for a college band to play and encourage alcohol abuse. Students protested loudly enough that the president reversed the ban and allows it to be played only after victories and on special occasions.

If you want to sing along—the verses alternate between instrumental and vocal—you'll need to learn it by ear. That's what the band does. There isn't any sheet music available.

Visiting Iowa

Originally the Iowa state capital (it lost the distinction to Des Moines in 1857), Iowa City is predominately a college town. You see evidence of that all over. Iowa is ranked number 8 on the list of U.S. party schools, and a trip up-and-down the Pedestrian Mall at night will give you a taste of why (literally and

figuratively). While not a reason for the ranking, Hamburg Inn No. 2 is a popular spot for people running for president before the Iowa caucuses. It was even featured on an episode of *The West Wing*. (It's called Hamburg Inn No. 2, by the way, since the original burned down.)

Where to Stay

❶ **Alexis Park Inn & Suites:** Located less than a mile from campus, this aviation themed hotel has 27 enormous suites in 3 separate buildings, and a B&B approach to hospitality. The buildings resemble a hotel/motel blended with a Swiss chalet from the outside. Inside, the one-, two-, and three-bedroom suites usually have Jacuzzis, and come with full kitchens, aviation-themed artwork and memorabilia, even some spare airplane parts (in case yours broke on the way in?). Suites run $100–$180 during football weekends, with a two-night minimum stay. (*(888) 925-3947, alexisparkinn.com*) ❷ **The Brown Street Inn:** This 1913 Gambrel Cottage–style mansion is on a quiet road in the Brown Street Historical District, and also near campus. The inn has five rooms and one suite. Each is spacious and comes with a private bath, wireless Internet connection, cable TV, and phone. During weekdays breakfast is an expanded continental style, while weekends add a hot entrée to the menu. Rooms run $75–$100 with a two-night minimum during football weekends. (*(319) 338-0435, brownstreetinn.com*) ❸ **Colony Country Campground:** Close to I-80 and closer to campus, this attractive campground has 45 RV sites with full hookups. There are no WiFi, cable TV, or phone hookups, but there are mature trees, gravel drives and sites, and lots of peace and quiet. Their bath facilities are clean, if a little outdated. Sites are $25. (*(319) 626-2221*) ❹ **The Golden Haug:** You get three buildings to choose from at this attractive and "pun-ny" B&B, just steps away from campus. The main house has five piggy-themed rooms, with names like "Swine and Roses" and "Cupig's VIP Caper." A second house, the Inn, has five extravagant suites, while the guesthouse has four homey rooms suited for more extended stays. The thematic suites cost more, but go fast, so call ahead for those. Breakfast is a gourmet affair, unless you stay in the guesthouse—breakfast is not part of the package at the guesthouse. Rooms and suites run from $100 to $175, with a two-night minimum stay during football weekends. (*(319) 354-4284, goldenhaug.com*) ❺ **hotelVetro:** This stylish downtown hotel offers studio suites outfitted with clean-lined Scandinavian

décor in tones of cream, gray, and brown, with birch wood accents. Suites are large and come with pillow-topped beds, sleeper sofa, plasma TV, high-speed Internet, oversized bathrooms, and well-equipped kitchenettes. All this can be yours for $279–$399 during football weekends. (*(800) 592-0355, hotelvetro.com*)

❻ **Iowa House Hotel:** Located on campus, Iowa House sits on the banks of the Iowa River offering 100 rooms and suites, many with riverside views. The décor isn't anything unusual, but you'll get either dial-up or Ethernet Internet access, along with cable TV. There's also a health club on the property. On football weekends rooms run $130, suites from $150–$270. (*(319) 335-3513, iowahousehotel.com*)

Where to Eat

TAILGATE SUPPLIES: ❶ **Iowa City Farmer's Market:** From May until the last days of October, this outdoor market provides shoppers with produce, herbs and sauces, meats, and baked goods, plus some handcrafted goods. Located on the lower level of the Chauncey Swan parking ramp, the market's open Wednesdays and Saturdays. (*(319) 356-5110*)

SPORTS BARS: ❷ **The Fieldhouse:** This bar has been a UI fixture since 1975, and has been featured in *Playboy*. Its interior is filled with Hawkeye artifacts and memorabilia, like Tim Dwight–autographed footballs, autographed jerseys, and photos of famous Iowa wrestlers. It's also littered with 58 TVs, including 3 big-screen and 4 projection-screen TVs. Toss in two pool tables and video games on the second level, and one of the state's biggest dance floors on its bottom level, and there's room enough for everyone. (*$, (319) 339-1516*)

RESTAURANTS: ❸ **The Brown Bottle:** Close to campus, this restaurant has built its reputation on rustic, flavor-packed fare. The menu is stocked with familiar, classic Italian dishes like veal Marsala, seafood lasagna, and garlic chicken, all prepared from scratch. Their gourmet pizzas are also local favorites. The interior is simple, with little of the clichéd décor sometimes found in Italian restaurants. (*$, (319) 351-6704, iowacitybrownbottle.com*) ❹ **Devotay:** It's Iowa's first tapas bar, featuring paella and a truckload of tapas, along with sandwiches and entrées, and a great wine list. Whether you're talking about the pork "Osso Buco," grilled chorizo, or their handmade plates, bowls, and cups, the word you're looking for is genuine. Whenever possible, Devotay gets all its

ingredients from local, sustainable sources. Inside the feeling is colorful and inviting. (*$, (319) 354-1001, devotay.net*) ❺ **Iowa River Power Company:** This restaurant proudly serves what they swear are Iowa's best steaks, and that's in a state famous for its beef. Housed in a former mill in nearby Coralville, the Power Company is perched on the banks of the Iowa River, giving diners a striking view of its waters. Try a slab of prime rib, one of several surf-n-turf combinations, or the grilled duck or fresh tuna steaks. (*$$, (319) 351-1904, powercompanyrestaurant.com*) ❻ **The Red Avocado:** Iowa City's only all-organic restaurant, this little café is an oasis of natural food in the heart of the beef country. This laid back café offers an inventive selection of vegan dishes including mushroom-walnut pate and sweet potato gnocchi, with roasted red peppers and vegetable-tomato sauce. Lunchtime features a choice of sandwiches, soups, and burritos. (*$, (319) 351-6088, theredavocado.com*)

Daytime Fun

❶ **Amana Colonies:** About a half-hour drive from Iowa City is a community of social and historical significance. While often confused with the Amish, the Amana Colonies were founded in 1854 by a group of German Inspirationists who moved to Iowa from Buffalo, New York, for economic and religious reasons. *Amana* is a word from the Old Testament that means "to remain faithful," and the community has remained faithful to its faith and lifestyle. Until 1932 all the land and buildings in the Amana villages were owned by the community. Families were assigned living quarters and adults worked at assigned tasks in the kitchens, fields, factories, or shops. There are several tours of historic sites here, along with shopping, dining, entertainment, and arts that relate back to the community's origin. You can also hit the links on the 18-hole championship golf course. (*Free–$$, (800) 579-2294, amanacolonies.com*) ❷ **Antique Car Museum of Iowa:** There're some old tailgates here. Cars from the 1890s to the 1990s showcase how technology and design have changed what we take to the parking lot on game day—and to the store and work every other day. In addition to the vehicles, there's a restored Skelly Gas Station, memorabilia, and a collection of unusual spark plugs for real gear-heads. (*$, (319) 354-3310*) ❸ **Devionian Fossil Gorge:** In 1993 Coralville Lake flooded and rushing waters overflowed the park. When the water receded, tons of dirt, a road, trees, and more were washed away. What it uncovered was a Devionian sea bed 375

million years old. How old is that? Well, dinosaurs wouldn't walk on the planet for another 200 million years. Fossils were revealed standing in relief and scientists began exploring this archeological treasure. Now the gorge is a park with tour paths through "Discovery Points" that explain the areas history and significance. (*Free, (319) 338-3543, mvr.usace.army.mil/Coralville/devonian_fossil_gorge.htm*) ❹ **Herbert Hoover Presidential Library & Museum:** Herbert Hoover was the nation's 31st president and the only Iowan to live in the White House. The museum walks visitors through Hoover's life and presidency with a collection of manuscripts, photographs, and oral histories. The cottage where Hoover was born and the gravesite of the president and his wife are also on the property. (*$, (319) 643-5301, hoover.nara.gov/index.html*)

Nighttime Fun

❶ **Brothers Bar & Grill:** Top 40 dance tunes drive the dance floor and Iowa students drive the social scene at this popular college bar. The only downside is it's not a big place, and it gets crowded, but isn't that what college bars are supposed to be like? (*$, (319) 338-6373*) ❷ **Deadwood:** An Iowa City institution since 1969 (although it's changed addresses some over the years), Deadwood is a unique and popular place with students and locals alike. For starters there's a dolphin hanging from the ceiling. Next, they call happy hour "Angry Hour." Legend has it Hunter S. Thompson was thrown out of the place. But it's this personality that has people camping out here for hours to eat, drink, and socialize. Some even study here. (*$, (319) 351-9417, deadwoodic.com*)

❸ **Iowa City Piano Lounge:** If you're looking for something laid back and off the beaten path, then this just might be your place. The music isn't all piano either, with acoustic guitar and other acts taking the stage. (*$, (319) 351-1797, thepianolounge.com/iowacity.html*) ❹ **The Picador:** It used to be called Gabes Oasis, but new owners meant a new name. But it's still one of Iowa City's favorite places to listen to live music. Mostly local and regional bands play here, but a national act will stop by now and then. Plenty of drink specials. (*$, (319) 354-4788, thepicador.com*)

Shopping

❶ **Antique Mall of Iowa City:** Appealing to both casual shoppers and serious collectors, the mall has vendors selling a wide variety of collectables, furniture, documents, and more. (*(319) 354-1822*) ❷ **Iowa Hawk Shop:** The name gives it away, but this is the official university shop for all things Hawkeye. You'll find everything from tailgate gear to beaded ankle bracelets. The Iowa Football Player Night-Light can keep you spirited and feeling secure too. There are five locations; the main store is on Highway 6 West. (*(800) HAWKSHOP, hawkshop.com*) ❸ **Iowa Artisans Gallery:** Located in the city's Old Capital Cultural District, the gallery began as a place for 12 local artists to display and sell their works. It's grown, and now you can view and buy works in media ranging from paint to metal to glass, and more. Iowa Artisans has been named a "Top 100 Retailer of American Crafts" 2 years in a row by *Niche Magazine*. (*(877) 439-6554, iowa-artisans-gallery.com*)

MICHIGAN

University of Michigan: 37,197 students
Ann Arbor, MI: pop. 114,024
Michigan Stadium: seats 107,501
Colors: Maize and Blue
Nickname: Wolverines
Mascot: None
Phone: (734) 647-9977, (734) 994-2330,
Pioneer High School

RVs park in Pioneer High School's Purple Lot, $150 for weekend. Season reserved RV pass holders can park 5 p.m. Friday; non-reserved RVs park Saturday 6 a.m., $125 for weekend. More RV parking at Varsity Tennis Center in Brown Lot, Friday arrivals $80 per weekend, Saturday (8 a.m.) arrivals $30; both stay 'til Sunday. Cars park in Brown Lot, Driving Range Lot, both $15. Shuttles available, $4 round trip. Tailgating starts 8 a.m. Saturday, continues through game. No alcohol in Pioneer High School lot.

Shuttle Info: Ann Arbor Transit Authority (theride.org) offers The Football Ride between Michigan Stadium and Ann Arbor hotels and motels, UM parking areas, the Michigan Union, and downtown. It costs $2 one way, $4 round trip per person. It runs every 20 minutes, starting 2 hours before kickoff, dropping off fans at Gate 2. Shuttles run for 1 hour postgame. During rain or heavy snow, the shuttle runs throughout the game.

Wolverines Media Partners: 1050-AM WTKA, 800-AM CKLW, 104.3-FM WOMC

There's a plot of land in Detroit that the Michigan Territory received as a condition of the Treaty of Fort Meigs from the Chippewa, Ottawa, and Potawatomi peoples. It was on that land in 1817 the legislature intended to build the newly established University of Michigan.

Not long after that, 40 acres was set aside in Ann Arbor, Michigan, by

locals who hoped the new state capital would be built there. It wasn't (Lansing got the honor) so they offered the land to the university instead.

The school took them up on it. In 1837 the land in Detroit was sold, and the university moved to Ann Arbor. Classes began on the new campus in 1841. It was a great student-teacher ratio: two professors and seven students. After the Civil War veterans began enrolling, and the student population was more than 1,200 by 1866. Four years later Michigan became the first major university to admit women as students.

In the late 19th and early 20th centuries, Michigan experienced significant academic growth adding programs in several fields including engineering and medicine. It now has more than 600 academic programs and is one of the nation's leading universities.

But more people know about Michigan because of football, not academics. That's what happens when you've won 42 Big Ten titles (a record for any team in any conference), 11 national titles, and have 3 Heisman Trophy winners (Tom Harmon in 1940, Desmond Howard in 1991, and Charles Woodson in 1997).

For the Wolverines it all started on May 30, 1879, with a 1–0 victory against Racine. For its first 11 years the team didn't have a coach but continued to win amassing a 23-1-1 record. In 1891 the team got its first coach—two, actually, who co-coached—and the squad went 4-5. But Michigan hasn't lost much since then.

There have been scores of great teams and coaches—too many to fit into this chapter—but they've led the Wolverines to the most wins and the highest winning percentage in Division-I history, the longest streak of winning seasons, the most undefeated seasons in Division-I football, and are one of only two schools to have a winning record against every conference in college football including independents, such as Notre Dame.

And about Notre Dame, it was the 1887 Wolverines that introduced football to the Fighting Irish, as the story goes. The team stopped by South Bend, Indiana, on the way to play Chicago and beat Notre Dame 8–0. Since then, the two have had one of America's storied rivalries.

While there have been many great Michigan coaches, one coach—Bo Schembechler—stands out. He coached in Ann Arbor from 1969 to 1989, winning 13 Big Ten titles and more games (234) than any other Michigan coach. His teams never had a losing season. He is considered one of the greatest coaches the college game has ever seen.

Schembechler also served as Michigan's athletic director and, after his retirement from the school, as president of the Detroit Tigers from 1990 to 1992.

Michigan plays in the "Big House"—also known as Michigan Stadium. It's the largest football-only stadium in the world and seats 107,501, although as many as 112,000 have been known to squeeze in for big games.

That "extra" seat that makes the stadium's capacity 107,501 is permanently reserved for Fielding Yost, who was athletic director when Fritz Crisler was coach (1938–1947). Crisler asked for the seat to be permanently reserved for his friend, and legend has it the coach was the only one who knew where that extra seat was.

School Mascot

The University of Michigan doesn't have a mascot, but it does have one of the most recognizable helmets in football. And it doesn't have anything to do with the nickname.

The winged helmet was the invention of coach Fritz Crisler in 1938. He replaced the old black helmets with it as a visual reminder of the new era of Michigan football he was bringing in. He also thought it would help his quarterback see receivers down field.

And if you're wondering what a wolverine is, it's a weasel. It's the second largest species of the weasel family and very strong for its size. They are known,

among other things, for their ability to kill animals much larger than they are.

How the wolverine came to represent the school is up for debate. They are not animals found in Michigan—never have been—but the term was first used in relation to the university around 1861.

One theory for the name's use is because wolverine pelts were traded in the area during the state's early days. Another is because the French settled the area and their appetites were judged to be gluttonous like wolverines'. A third is that the moniker comes from a border dispute with Ohio in the early 1800s—although it's not sure if Michigan used the term to show their strength, or if Ohio used it to describe Michigan's aggressive behavior.

There have been a few live wolverines used as mascots through the years, most recently in the late 1930s. But the university does not sanction a live mascot today, and never has recognized any of

Michigan Fight Song

"The Victors"

Now for a cheer they are here, triumphant!
Here they come with banners flying,
In stalwart step they're nighing,
With shouts of vict'ry crying,
We hurrah, hurrah, we greet you now,
Hail!

Far we their praises sing
For the glory and fame they've bro't us
Loud let the bells them ring
For here they come with banners flying
Far we their praises tell
For the glory and fame they've bro't us
Loud let the bells them ring
For here they come with banners flying
Here they come, Hurrah!

Hail! to the victors valiant
Hail! to the conqu'ring heroes
Hail! Hail! to Michigan
The leaders and best
Hail! to the victors valiant
Hail! to the conqu'ring heroes
Hail! Hail! to Michigan,
The champions of the West!

We cheer them again
We cheer and cheer again
For Michigan, we cheer for Michigan
We cheer with might and main
We cheer, cheer, cheer
With might and main we cheer!

Hail! to the victors valiant
Hail! to the conqu'ring heroes
Hail! Hail! to Michigan,
The champions of the West!

"The Yellow and Blue"

Sing to the colors that float in the light;
Hurrah for the Yellow and Blue!
Yellow the stars as they ride through the night
And reel in a rollicking crew;
Yellow the fields where ripens the grain
And yellow the moon on the harvest wain;
Hail!
Hail to the colors that float in the light
Hurrah for the Yellow and Blue!

Blue are the billows that bow to the sun
When yellow robed morning is due.
Blue are the curtains that evening has spun
The slumbers of Phoebus to woo;
Blue are the blossoms to memory dear
And blue is the sapphire and gleams like a tear;
Hail!
Hail to the ribbons that nature has spun;
Hurrah for the Yellow and Blue!

the costumed mascots proposed during the decades.

Game-Day Traditions
The Rock

It's a huge boulder planted at Washtenaw and Hills Streets in 1932 to commemorate George Washington's 200th birthday. Now it's The Rock—a Michigan tradition protected during football season from vandals like Buckeyes and Spartans who would paint it rival colors.

The first paint job was gray, but it has worn many colors during the past 6 decades. Sometimes opposing fans have suc-cessfully repainted The Rock, but more often than not, Michigan stu-dents have preserved The Rock's honor. It is also used to honor others, like the time it was painted in tribute to those who died on 9/11.

Visiting Michigan

Since 1837, when the University of Michigan moved here from Detroit, this has been a college town. The campus and the city have had a reputation for liberal leanings.

Ann Arbor was a stop on the Underground Railroad during the Civil War. Later, during the 1960s and 1970s, President John F. Kennedy unveiled his Peace Corps here, and President Lyndon Johnson used Ann Arbor as the stage to propose his Great Society program.

Where to Stay

❶ **Ann Arbor Bed and Breakfast:** Built in 1962, this contemporary chalet is right next to campus. There are nine guestrooms with private baths, most of which have a private patio or balcony; two of the rooms have kitchenettes. It's also one of the few B&Bs with covered parking. Staying here will set you back $129–$159. (*(734) 994-9100, annarborbedandbreakfast.com*) ❷ **Bell Tower Hotel:** Old World elegance and its English style are two reasons why this hotel won the Outstanding Historic Preservation award. The hotel offers rooms and suites, and if you need a gym you can use the University of Michigan's fitness facility. Rates run $191–$297. (*(800) 562-3559, belltowerhotel.com*) ❸ **KC Campground:** KC offers 100 sites in a country setting about 10 minutes from Ann Arbor, in Milan. The campground also has picnic areas, arcade,

playground, swimming pool, and bath house. There's also a small camp store on-site. Sites run $25. (*(734) 439-1076, kccampgroundmilan.com*) ❹ **KOA Detroit/Greenfield:** On a private spring-fed lake in Ypsilanti, this campsite offers 207 sites, fishing, mini golf, and groceries. Don't plan on doing your tailgate menu shopping here, but you can pick up some last-minute items. Sites cost $30–$36. It's a KOA, so Kamping Kabins are also available. (*(734) 482-7722, koa.com/where/mi/22178*) ❺ **Lamp Post Inn:** Rooms at the inn have microwave ovens and refrigerators, or a full kitchenette. Located near campus, they say 90 percent of their guests are repeat customers, so they're doing something right. Rooms cost $45–$60 or $75–$90 when there are events in town. (*(734) 971-8000, lamppostinn.com*) ❻ **Parish House Inn:** Located in nearby Ypsilanti, this Queen Ann–style house had been named one of the top 15 B&Bs located near a college or university by *Inn Traveler Magazine*. There are eight guest rooms with private baths. You can also enjoy the river-walk garden on the property. Rooms run $93–$165. (*(800) 480-4866, parishhouseinn.com*)

Where to Eat

TAILGATE SUPPLIES:

❶ Zingerman's Deli: It's an Ann Arbor institution and a great place to find hearth-baked breads, farmhouse cheeses, estate-bottled olive oils, smoked fish, salami, coffee, tea, and more. Located near the year-round Ann Arbor Farmers' Market (where you can find other tailgate supplies, too). (*(734) 663-3354, zingermans.com*)

SPORTS BARS: **❷ The Arena Sports Bar:** This is Ann Arbor's "Restaurant of Champions" (it says so on the logo). Those champions are able to watch the game on several TVs, and choose from a menu that features the expected burgers and bar food, but also seafood, pasta, and steak. (*$, (734) 222-9999, thearenasportsbar.com*) **❸ Enzo's Sports Bar & More:** More than 20 TVs—including 3 projection screens—means you can see the game from most anywhere at Enzo's. You can also play pool and video games. In addition to sports and food, live bands take the stage many nights. (*$, (734) 665-1600, enzossportsbarandmore.com*)

RESTAURANTS: **❹ Aubree's:** You can come for dinner, stay for games, and finish up with a nightcap in this historic 1870s building in Ypsilanti. You'll enjoy a variety of dishes at Aubree's on the first floor. Locals will tell you to try the burgers and pasta. Head up the stairs and you'll find **Sticks Pool & Pub**, where you can, well, play pool and drink. One more level up is the **Tiki Rooftop Bar**. Tiki's opens in March and shuts down when it's just too cold to be on a roof in

Michigan. (*$, (734) 483-1870, aubrees.com*) ❺ **Bella Ciao:** Regional Italian fare is on the menu, alongside a wine list that also explores the country's regions. You'll find traditional dishes mixed in with some creative twists. The lobster ravioli is a favorite here. (*$$, (734) 995-2107, bellaciao.com*) ❻ **Zingerman's Roadhouse:** You'll find burgers and steaks, pasta, and salads, but the star of the show is the fish. Fish you don't see on menus that much—such as escolar, shad, and walleye—share space with those you see more often, like salmon. The Zingermans also have a deli, bakehouse, coffee operation, and more in Ann Arbor. (*$, (734) 663-3663, zingermansroadhouse.com*)

Daytime Fun

❶ **Matthaei Botanical Gardens & Nichols Arboretum:** You may be in Michigan, but here you'll visit three other climates: tropical rainforest, Mediterranean, and desert. Those are all in the conservatory. Outside on the Gardens' 300 acres you'll experience outdoor display gardens and miles of nature trails. Nestled into the hills next to the central campus is The Nichols Arboretum, a 123-acre living museum. (*$, (734) 998-7060, sitemaker.umich.edu/mbgna*) ❷ **Michigan Firehouse Museum:** From horse-drawn pumps to bright red fire engines, the Ypsilanti museum preserves Michigan's firefighting history and promotes fire safety. Exhibits also include bells, equipment, and toy fire trucks. (*$, (734) 547-0663, michiganfirehousemuseum.org*) ❸ **University of Michigan Museum of Art:** With works from Picasso to Rembrandt, Whistler to Cézanne, this is considered one of the top 10 university art museums in the country. Exhibits also include African sculpture, contemporary photography, and a Japanese gallery. Note: Its permanent location (Alumni Memorial Hall) is undergoing renovation, so until mid-2008 the museum is in a temporary location adjacent to campus. (*Free, (734) 764-0395, umma.umich.edu*)

Nighttime Fun

❶ **Conor O'Neill's:** This is a real Irish Pub. It was designed and built in Ireland, then shipped to Ann Arbor. The food on the menu is just as Irish, as is the beer— Guinness, Murphy's, and Newcastle are on tap. There's also traditional Irish music on Sundays. (*$, (734) 665-2968, conoroneills.com*) ❷ **Divine:** This is Ypsilanti's hip nightspot. You've got DJs playing dance music, theme nights, a bar (of course), and a VIP Lounge upstairs. (*(734) 485-4444, club-divine.com*) ❸ **Firefly Club:** Firefly is all about live jazz and blues. You can hear it here every night of the week. It also has the feel of an old jazz club, including the exposed

brick walls. The bar is fully stocked, but the kitchen serves a limited menu. (*(734) 665-9090, fireflyclub.com*)

Shopping

❶ **Kerrytown District:** Just north of downtown Ann Arbor, this is where you'll find the Farmers' Market and the Artisan Market, as well as other shops, restaurants, galleries, and a children's museum. (*kerrytown.org*)   ❷ **Main Street and State Street:** Along these blocks near the University of Michigan and in the downtown area are a variety of shops, eateries, galleries, and museums. Go to the Web site to print coupons for many downtown merchants. (*mainstreetannarbor.org, a2state.com*)   ❸ **Ulrich's Bookstore:** If it's maize, blue or has an *M* on it, you'll find it here. Ulrich's Spirit Shop is stocked full of Michigan stuff for your body, your car, your home, your friends, your tailgate . . . you get the idea. (*(734) 662-3201, ulrichs.com*)

MICHIGAN STATE

Michigan State University: 43,159 students
East Lansing, MI: pop. 46,525
Spartan Stadium: seats 72,027
Colors: Green and White
Nickname: Spartans
Mascot: Sparty
Phone: (517) 355-8440

RVs park in lots across from the Grounds Department and in Physical Plant Parking Lot, for $30. No overnight parking. Tailgating starts 7 a.m., 9 a.m., or 1 p.m. depending on time of game. Lawn or outdoor furniture only. No kegs or beer balls. No drinking game gear. No trailers, including pig roasters. Oversized trucks park in RV parking. Dispose of all trash properly. No canopies over 10 x 10 feet. Munn Field available for alcohol-free tailgating.

Shuttle Info: Green Line available at Lot 89, $3 round trip.

Spartans Media Partners: 1240-AM WJIM, 94.9-FM WMMQ

Michigan State was founded after a legislated battle with the president of the University of Michigan to teach the science and practice of agriculture to the sons of the state's farmers (Michigan wanted the school to be part of its Ann Arbor campus' curriculum). The school—which was first called the Agricultural College of the State of Michigan—was the country's first agricultural college. Its first class was admitted in 1857, but the school lost almost all its students when they left to enlist in the Union Army in 1861. That first class was graduated in absentia.

During the war the nation's first agricultural college found itself a national leader again. While it is a technical, political, and administrative story of which state board controlled the school, the end result was MSU became

the Pioneer Land Grant College after President Abraham Lincoln signed the Morrill Act in 1862 granting federal lands to state universities. Michigan State's system was used as the model for other states' educational systems.

At the end of the 19th century, the school admitted its first female students (1870) and first African-American student (1899). The school's biggest growth came after World War II, thanks to the G.I. Bill, when enrollment tripled at Michigan State College of Agriculture and Applied Science (the name was changed to the simpler Michigan State University in 1964).

The end of the 19th century is also when football found its way to campus. It had been a club sport since 1884, but the first official team took the field in 1896. The early Spartan teams were pretty good ones, but the program got big with Biggie.

Biggie Munn took over coaching duties in 1947 and began building what some called the nation's leading football factory of the time. His first couple of seasons were building years, but an otherwise nondescript win over William & Mary in 1950 was the first of what would become a school-record 28 straight wins, lasting until his retirement from coaching in 1953. Under Biggie's leadership the Spartans won the biggest title of all: the 1952 national championship (although he would later say he felt the 1951 team was better).

When he left the sidelines to take over as Michigan State's athletic director, he took with him a .857 winning percentage—still the best of any Spartan head coach. He left the team to his assistant, Duffy Daugherty, who coached MSU until 1972, including the Spartans' other national championship in 1965. He is also the man who said, "Football isn't a contact sport, it's a collision sport. Dancing is a contact sport."

Michigan State has also put some great players on the field, including Larry Bethea, Charlie Rogers, Bubba Smith, Brad Van Pelt, and Lorenzo White. There are two Spartans in the Pro Football Hall of Fame: Herb Adderley and Joe DeLamielleure.

School Mascot

Being an agricultural school, Michigan State's first teams were called the Aggies. That all changed in 1925 when the school had grown into other fields of curriculum and felt it needed a new nickname. The contest winner: Michigan Staters.

That didn't sit too well with a couple of sports writers at the two Lansing papers; they felt the winning name wasn't suitable for newspaper headlines. So they looked over the other contest entries and decided Spartans was a better choice and started using the name. Ah, the power of the press.

There have been several versions of the Spartan mascot over the years. The costumed one with the big head was introduced in 1989. In addition to fans, Sparty is popular with ESPN—he's been in several of the network's commercials. Sparty's

also popular with contest judges; in 2004 and 2005 he was crowned "Best Mascot."

Game-Day Traditions
Sparty Watch

The bronze statue on campus of the Spartan warrior was the first Sparty—nicknamed not long after it was created by assistant art professor Leonard Jungwirth in 1941. (The bronze statue was actually made in 2005, replacing the original terra cotta statue that was deteriorating. It is on display inside Spartan Stadium.)

It's a tradition for students and alumni to have their picture taken with Sparty. It's also a tradition for rivals to try and paint him *their* school colors. Especially archrival Michigan. So Sparty Watch also became a tradition.

For the entire week of a Michigan game at MSU, members of the Spartan Marching Band guard the statue round-the-clock to prevent vandals from getting close enough to do any damage. During the week other students, including some football players and coaches, will stop by offering support and, perhaps more important, food for the faithful guards.

Visiting Michigan State

About the same time Lansing became the state capital, in 1847, the settlement that grew into East Lansing was founded, although the post office address was

"Agricultural College, Michigan" (which is what Michigan State was originally called). East Lansing is a pretty typical college town (almost 60 percent of the population is between 18–24 years old), although its relationship with university students has been rocky at times. Nonetheless, the growth of East Lansing has paralleled the growth of MSU since the university is the area's primary economic driver and employer.

Where to Stay

❶ **The English Inn:** About 15 minutes from East Lansing, this Tudor-style inn offers six large guestrooms, two cottages, and two suites. Rooms are nicely decorated and feature private baths, cable TV, antique

furnishings, and views of the extensive grounds. Unlike many B&Bs, this inn comes with a lot of extras for guests, like a swimming pool, croquet court, and free reign to explore the perennial gardens, riverside trails, and fishpond. There's also an award-winning restaurant here. Rooms run $105–$175. (*(800) 858-0598, englishinn.com*)

❷ **Kellogg Hotel & Conference Center:** Located on MSU's campus, this hotel's rooms are European-sized (a little smaller than American) but clean and in good shape; they come equipped with cable TV and wired and wireless Internet connections. The hotel's décor is traditional, without being cookie-cutter. During football weekends, rooms run $129–$169, suites run $365–$494. The hotel also serves a popular Sunday brunch. (*(800) 875-5090, kelloggcenter.com*) ❸ **Lansing Cottonwood Campground:** Located in the heart of Lansing, this campground has 142 sites. Full hookups are available at 11 sites; there's water and electric only at 99 sites, and 35 sites are dry (no hookups). You won't find cable, phone, or Internet hookups here, but you will find the grounds are well kept, and all facilities are clean. There's also a pond. Rates run from $20 for a dry site to $27.50 for one with full hookups. Call ahead to reserve sites with hookups to be sure you get one. (*(517) 393-3200, lansingcottonwoodcampground.com*) ❹ **Topliff's Tara Bed & Breakfast:** It's a B&B and a llama farm. Really. Located in the bedroom community of Williamston, Topliff's Tara sits on a 50-acre llama farm (if the weather's nice, you can visit the llamas, or even take one on a hike with you). The home, built in 1905, offers five cozy guestrooms, each with its own theme. Two rooms have private baths; the rest share facilities. Rates run $75–$140, based on the room and if single or double occupancy. (*(517) 655-8860, topliffstara.com*) ❺ **Wild Goose Inn:** This B&B is just two blocks from campus and has six suites, located in two houses (the Wild Goose and the Gosling). The houses are connected by a shared deck with a gas fire pit. Rooms are imaginatively decorated, and come equipped with a private bath, fireplace, and cable TV with DVD/CD player. All rooms, save one, have Jacuzzis. Rooms run $129–$159, with a two-night minimum stay during football season. (*(517) 333-3334, wildgooseinn.com*)

Where to Eat

TAILGATER SUPPLIES: ❶ **Foods for Living:** They have your menu covered from frozen foods, fresh meats, and cheeses to a deli, vegetarian fare, and even pre-packaged local restaurant food. You'll also find herbs, fruits, and organic vegetables, and some unusual do-it-yourself opportunities, like making your own peanut butter from their peanuts.

(*(517) 324-9010*) ❷ **Meijer Superstore:** This regional chain superstore is still family owned and stocks Michigan produce whenever possible. A great "one-stop" shop and a real experience for out-of-staters, Meijer invented the superstore concept, beating Wal-Mart to the punch by 26 years. A typical Meijer superstore carries more than 150,000 items. Yeah, you'll probably find what you need. (*(517) 332-2444, meijer.com*)

SPORTS BARS: ❸ **Nuthouse Sports Grill:** Next to Oldsmobile Park, this friendly sports pub is a

favorite with Spartan fans. Watch the game on Nuthouse's numerous TVs or three state-of-the-art, large-screen HD projectors. The food here isn't your average bar food; try their Hawaiian chicken with mango salsa, grilled salmon with dill sauce, Tex-Mex, grinders, and calzones. With 14 beers on tap, pool tables, arcade games, megatouch, pinball, and theme nights, there's always a crowd. (*$, (517) 484-NUTS, nuthousesportsgrill.com*) ❹ Spartan Sports Den: It's one of the best places in East Lansing to catch MSU sporting events on the tube. A 56-inch projection TV in the back airs big games, and eight smaller, 32-inch sets are scattered about, making it easy to catch the game from just about any table or barstool. The kitchen serves up typical pub cuisine, with their hamburgers rated a perennial favorite. Those needing to work off some adrenaline can take on friends in a few games of eight ball. NTN Trivia is also available. (*$, (517) 333-1944*) ❺ Tripper's Sports Bar: They say this is Mid-Michigan's biggest sports bar. For starters, it has 50 TVs stationed in every nook and cranny. MSU fans also flock here to hear head football coach Bobby Williams and men's basketball coach Tom Izzo broadcast their radio shows from the bar. Tripper's also provides pool tables, dartboards, and the Arena, where you'll find free-throw shooting machines, motorcycle and car simulators, and video arcade games. And they have food, too—everything from prime rib au jus and teriyaki salmon, to fat burgers and brats with sauerkraut. (*$–$$, (517) 336-0717*)

RESTAURANTS: ❻ **Beggar's Banquet:** Named for the Rolling Stones album, Beggar's has plenty of mojo to spare. Parts of its walls are old barn wood, the bar was once a lane from a bowling alley, and the stained glass windows were taken from a dismantled church and pieced back together. The restaurant offers a menu of seasonally changing American favorites like maple-Dijon pork medallions or a spinach and dried cherry salad, with walnuts, bleu cheese, and poppy seed vinaigrette. (*$–$$, (517) 351-4573, beggarsbanquet.com*)
❼ **SanSu:** Voted "Best of the Best Sushi" in 2006 by the *Lansing State Journal*, this restaurant offers the largest and freshest sushi and sashimi in town. Enjoy a variety of entrées from bento boxes to udon dishes and teriyaki dinners. The interior reflects Japan's traditionally understated, serene aesthetic, with a main dining area, sushi bar, and two private tatami rooms. (*$–$$, (517) 333-1933, sansu-sushi.com*) ❽ **Soup Spoon Café:** Located in Lansing, it's a great place for lunch, with cozy, dark red tables, wood chairs, and warm yellow walls. The

menu is a creative mix of foods and flavors, equally divided among hot and cold sandwiches, lunch entrées, and fresh salads—and soup, of course. Try the Voodoo pasta with Gulf shrimp and bell peppers with linguine in a Cajun cream sauce (and if you can say that fast 10 times, you're hired). (*$, (517) 316-2377*) ❾ **Traveler's Club International Restaurant & Tuba Museum:** I know,

it's an odd mix. But this is a quirky place. Just down the road in Okemos, this restaurant (and museum) was founded to give customers a chance to "travel" the world via international cuisine. The regular menu features Asian, Middle Eastern, and Latin sections, plus some burgers for the less adventurous. The specials menu features cuisine from a different continent each month. Weekly specials focus on specific countries with a prix fixe menu. Inside, a quirky combination of artifacts and fabrics decorates the walls. Then there are the tubas . . . some 30 of them highlighted by a rare 1915 Austrian beauty. Don't miss the "Sousafountain" gurgling on the back patio. (*$, (517) 349-1701, travelerstuba.com/travelersclub_001.htm*)

Daytime Fun

❶ **Country Mill:** The apple orchard's been here since 1871, but they didn't have the cider bar and petting zoo then. Or the bakery and pumpkin patch. Or the gift shop and other attractions at this family-owned farm. It's the only farm in middle Michigan where you can pick your own apples and pumpkins (unless you happen to own property with apple trees and a pumpkin patch). All the attractions and events are designed for families. You can get coupons and discounts on their

Web site. (*$, (517) 543-1019, countrymill.com*) ❷ **Horticulture Gardens at MSU:** If you're a gardener, or just enjoy gardens, then this is a must-stop on your trip. You can tour the various gardens or learn a trick or two from one of their experts. The Saturday Morning Gardener is a popular program; call ahead to see what programs are open while you're in town. (*$, (517) 355-5191, hrt.msu.edu/gardens/Index.htm*) ❸ **Kresge Art Museum:** Founded in 1959, the museum is on campus and includes works spanning more than 5,000 years—from ancient Cycladic figures to contemporary pieces in mixed media. Permanent and rotating exhibits explore everything from ancient marble Egyptian pieces to introspective American photography, and from Medieval paintings to circus art. (*Free, (517) 353-9834, artmuseum.msu.edu*)

❹ **MSU Bug House:** There are more kinds of beetles in Michigan than there are types of birds on earth. Sounds like a good reason to have a Bug House at MSU then. This shrine to everything creepy and crawly—at least of the insect variety—has more than a million specimens in its collection (they've been collecting since before the Civil War). In addition to the basics, you'll learn that crickets have ears on their knees, and a fly's taste buds are on its feet. Well, you won't learn that since I just told you and you know it now, but you get the idea. You'll need to plan ahead to visit the Bug House. It's open Monday evenings and limited afternoons

when school's in session. It costs $30 for a one-hour tour if your group is less than 30 people. (*$$–$$$, (517) 355-4662, ent.msu.edu/bughouse/index.html*)

Nighttime Fun

❶ **Crunchy's:** MSU students pack this place for its buckets of beer, entertainment (everything from comedy to karaoke), and just plain ole good times. The food is basic pub food but better prepared than most. Locals say it's *the* place to get burgers, and they have a good selection of local and regional beers at the bar. This is a college hangout, so expect a crowd and some noise. (*$, (517) 351-2506*)

❷ **The Exchange:** Live music every night, award-winning cocktails, and imported cigars make The Exchange a popular downtown Lansing night spot. The dancing and bands are downstairs; upstairs you'll find **The Terrace Lounge** with its big, cushy sofas and conversational atmosphere. (*$, (517) 319-4500, lansingexchange.com*) ❸ **Green Door Lounge:** If you ask someone where to listen to live jazz and blues, chances are they're going

to send you here. The Green Door usually sits atop Lansing's "Best of" lists for its live music six nights a week and lounge atmosphere, along with cheap beer and good food. It's located between campus and the state capitol so you get an interesting mix of people here, too. (*$, (517) 482-6376, greendoorlive.com*)

❹ **The Michigan Princess:** This Princess is a triple-deck river boat that weighs 100 tons and offers cruises up and down the river. The cruises board at Grand River Park and provide a leisurely journey for dining, dancing, or just relaxing and watching the shore go by. (*$$$, (517) 627-2154, michiganprincess.com*)

❺ **Peanut Barrel:** Yes, you can get peanuts here. You can also get sandwiches and roll-ups, and any of a couple dozen different beers. The Peanut Barrel is a comfortable college hangout for students and locals, with pool tables, arcade games, and some TVs to watch a game. Check out the hand-painted murals on the base of the bar. The outdoor patio is great when the weather's nice. (*$, (517) 351-0608, peanutbarrel.com*)   ❻ **Rick's American Café:** It's been voted *Playboy's* "College Bar of the Month," so you can guess the party atmosphere you'll find here. This is also one of the most popular places near campus to catch live music, and its dance floor is crowded most every night of the week. ($, *(517) 351-2285, ricksamericancafe.com*)

Shopping

❶ **Downtown East Lansing:** Stroll the tree-lined streets of downtown East Lansing and you'll find a number of galleries, gift shops, boutiques, and more. You'll find used books and music in several shops, too. If you're hungry you can stop at any number of places to grab a bite. (*cityofeastlansing.com*) ❷ **Student Book Store in East Lansing:** Need a MSU garden gnome? No problem. A Spartan hitch cover with bottle opener? Check. A plush Spartan mascot helmet? Got it. They also sell all the usual stuff in green and white. You'll find them on campus. (*(517) 351-4210, sbsmsu.com*)

MINNESOTA

University of Minnesota: 51,194 students
Minneapolis, MN: pop. 373,943
Hubert H. Humphrey Metrodome: seats 64,172
Colors: Maroon and Gold
Nickname: Golden Gophers
Mascot: Goldy Gopher
Phone: (612) 332-4735

RVs and tailgaters park in U of M Tailgating Lot, at Rapid Park, $12 per space used. Lot opens 4 hours before kickoff. No overnight parking. Free shuttle service provided. Not many restrictions—just bring lots of trash bags. Receptacles provided, and university will pick up bagged trash left behind.

Shuttle Info: Extensive, free shuttle service available, with five campus stops. Metrodome Shuttle Bus Service starts 1 3/4 hours before kickoff, with service every 5–7 minutes. The return shuttle runs until 45 minutes after game's end.

Golden Gophers Media Partners: 830-AM WCCO, 88.5-FM KBEM

While the University of Minnesota is a state university, it has some freedoms other state schools don't. That's because it was founded before there was a state.

Minnesota opened as a college preparatory school in 1851, 7 years before Minnesota joined the Union. But the preparatory school hit hard times during the Civil War, and financial struggles forced the school to close. It didn't reopen until 1867.

When it reopened the school was still in debt, but things were about to get better.

In 1868 the preparatory school became a university, and at about the same time, John Sargent Pillsbury became its financial angel.

Pillsbury was a successful Minneapolis politician and business man (yes, it's his surname that's the first name of that famous doughboy). He served as Minnesota's eighth governor, and with his finances and political clout, he helped the university pull out of debt. He later served as a regent for the school. For all of this he is known as "The Father of the University."

The school has grown a lot since then, of course, and today its Twin Cities campus is located in Minneapolis and St. Paul. The main campus sits on both banks of the Mississippi River in Minneapolis, and the school has become one of the nation's leading research universities.

If Pillsbury was "The Father of the University," you could make an argument that Henry Williams was "The Father of Minnesota Football," although he doesn't carry that nickname.

The school began playing football in 1882, but Williams was the Gophers' first full-time, paid coach when he took the helm in 1900. He led the team for 21 years compiling a 136-33-11 record. His teams won eight Big Ten titles and laid the groundwork for what became a very successful program during the next 30 years when the Gophers racked up several Big Ten titles and six national championships.

Williams's 1904 team was one for the record books. That team went 13-0, including what is still the most lopsided win in school history—a 146–0 walloping of Grinnell. Believe it or not, Minnesota scored 73 points in each half. How's that for a consistent game?

Thirty years later, under coach Bernie Bierman, Minnesota again went undefeated, winning the school's first national championship. They went on to three-peat, winning the title in 1934, 1935, and 1936. Bierman's team also won back-to-back championships in 1940 and 1941. In addition to the national championship, Bruce Smith won the 1941 Heisman Trophy. He's the only Gopher to win the coveted award and is arguably the best player to ever play at Minnesota.

But there's no argument that the 1960 team owns the biggest turnaround in school history, and one of the biggest ever in college football.

The 1959 Gophers were bad. They went 2-7 and finished last in the Big Ten. No one expected much more of them in 1960, but the team surprised everyone by finishing the season 8-2, earning Minnesota's first trip to the Rose Bowl, and being crowned national champions.

School Mascot

Minnesota is the Golden Gophers, but they weren't always golden. And Goldy Gopher doesn't look much like a gopher. I'll explain.

The whole gopher thing started in 1857 when a political cartoon ridiculing the Railroad Loan that helped open up the West depicted railroad barons as striped gophers pulling a railroad car filled with the Minnesota Territorial Legislature to the "Slough of Despond." During the next several years, Minnesota became known as the Gopher State, even though the illustrations of the gophers weren't really gophers. They were humanized characterizations of 13-striped ground squirrels. No one knows if the artist knew they weren't gophers. But the artist who made the identity crisis worse had an idea of what he was doing.

His name was George Grooms, and he was an artist for a small Iowa manufacturing company. When the school officially adopted the gopher mascot in 1940 (the name was first used in 1887 when the school's first yearbook was titled the *Gopher Annual* and quickly became the school's informal mascot), it hired Grooms to draw the official Gopher mascot.

The problem was he didn't know what a gopher looked like. As he made his way from Iowa to Minnesota he sketched drawings of various rodents he saw at rest stops. Some were squirrels; others were chipmunks. The resulting Minnesota Gopher looked more like a chipmunk than anything else.

The school never made that drawing official, so several variations of Goldy appeared. Incidentally, the name "Goldy" appeared sometime during the 1960s.

But even as several *official* mascots were created over the years (including an aggressive-looking one at the request of then football coach Lou Holtz), Goldy never got rid of the buck teeth and facial features of a chipmunk. Even the costumed mascot walking the stands at games—which first appeared in 1952—looks more like a cousin of Alvin and the Chipmunks than a gopher.

ALMA MATER

"Minnesota, Hail to Thee!"

Hail to thee, our college dear!
Thy light shall ever be
A beacon bright and clear
Thy sons and daughters true
Will proclaim thee near and far.
They will guard thy fame, and adore thy name;
Thou shalt be their Northern Star!

As for when the Gophers became Golden, that happened in the 1930s when the team wore all-gold uniforms and radio announcer Halsey Hall began referring to them as the Golden Gophers. The name stuck—the uniforms didn't. Later the university officially changed its nickname from the Gophers to the Golden Gophers.

Game-Day Traditions
Little Brown Jug

It started on Halloween in 1903 when Michigan coach Fielding Yost asked his student manager to buy a jug to hold water for when his Wolverines played at Minnesota that day. It was a 5-gallon, putty-colored jug that cost 30 cents.

Michigan was a powerhouse football squad, but the Gophers had one of their best teams in years, so they were excited about their chances that day. Michigan led the entire game, and it was 6–0 with just a few minutes left to play. But the Gophers struck and tied the game 6–6. Minnesota fans stormed the field to celebrate, even though there was still 2 minutes left in the game. But the crowd and an impending snow storm convinced the refs to call the game and Michigan left the field. Yost left his jug behind.

Minnesota took the jug, painted it brown, and wrote on it "Michigan Jug— Captured by Oscar, October 31, 1903, Michigan 6, Minnesota 6." (Oscar was Oscar

Munson, the custodian who found the jug on the field.)

Later, the legend goes, Yost asked for the jug back and was told, "We have your little brown jug; if you want it, you'll have to win it back." So began one of college football's longest-running trophy game rivalries.

Yost did get his jug back the next time they played. It's been Minnesota that's had the harder time keeping it. Michigan owns a 64-22-3 record in the series.

Visiting Minnesota

This is the City of Lakes. It's because of the 24 small lakes within the city that Minneapolis has its name. An early settler suggested the moniker, which is derived from the Dakota word for water (*mine*) and the Greek word for city (*polis*). Together with the Twin City of St. Paul, the state's capital, the metro area is home to more than 3 million people. The main campus area is on the east bank of the Mississippi River, and much of the action is in a four-block area known as the "Superblock." However, Minneapolis/St. Paul is known for great restaurants and entertainment, so you'll find things to do all over town.

Where to Stay

❶ **Elmwood House Bed & Breakfast:** This restored Normandy-style chateau was built in 1887 by noted architect Henry Wild Jones. There are four guestrooms furnished in distinctly European style; there's no Victorian fussiness, and a minimum of knickknacks. The first-floor living space is an example of Jones's trademark beamed ceilings and Inglenook fireplaces. Rooms run $75–$105. (*(612) 822-4558, elmwoodhouse.us*) ❷ **The Marquette Hotel:** This downtown Minneapolis boutique hotel is part of the IDS Center complex, an early 1970s, glass-front skyscraper designed by Philip Johnson. The Marquette has oversized rooms and suites, all stylishly furnished. Rates can vary greatly depending on time of year and occupancy level. During slower times rooms run $99–$239; at peak times rates jump to $315–$455. (*(612) 333-4545, marquettehotel.com*) ❸ **Minneapolis Northwest KOA:** Located in Rogers, about a half hour north of the Metrodome, this KOA has 80 sites with full hookups. Sites are average in size, with sunny and shady spots available. Wireless Internet is available, but cable TV and phone hookups aren't. Rates are $28–$38. (*(800) 562-0261, koa.com/where/mn/23113/*) ❹ **Nicollet Island Inn:** This 1893 limestone inn is on Nicollet Island, in the middle of the Mississippi River. The 24 individually decorated guestrooms are furnished with offbeat originality in shades of cream, taupe, and gold. All offer VCRs and freshly baked cookies; some have Jacuzzis. The inn's restaurant has garnered many regional and national awards. While this is an inn, B&B style packages are available. Rooms run $200–$260, depending on the room and when you stay. (*(612) 331-*

1800, nicolletislandinn.com)

❺ Wales House: Filled with attractive antiques this fully furnished, 10-bedroom home is endowed with a homey atmosphere. Many of Wales's guests are visiting faculty and scholars, often from abroad, adding some erudite conversation to your stay. Some rooms share baths; some have private baths. If you share a bath, a night will cost you $55; those with private baths pay $10 more. (*(612) 331-3931, waleshouse.com*)

Where to Eat

TAILGATER SUPPLIES: **❶ Minneapolis Farmers' Market:** This is Minnesota's largest open-air, covered market, open 7 days a week. It's big enough to have two locations: the main market on Lyndale Avenue and an additional site nearby at Nicollet Mall. You'll find both sites crammed with vendors selling produce, meats, and other foodstuffs. If you're looking for a centerpiece for your tailgate, there's a variety of cut and potted flowers and other plants. (*(612) 333-1718, mplsfarmersmarket.com*) **❷ Wedge Co-op:** Called "The Wedge" by Twin Cities residents, this snazzy food co-op is listed in "Best 100 Things about the Twin Cities" by *Minneapolis/St. Paul Magazine*. Not only does this brick, wedge-shaped store look cool, it's full of top-quality food products at prices reasonable for customers, and fair to growers. (*(612) 871-3993, wedge.coop/index.html*)

SPORTS BARS: **❸ Stub & Herb's:** A University of Minnesota mainstay, this 60-year-old bar has vintage megaphones and pennants hanging from the bar, while photos of Gopher triumphs and other U of M and Big Ten memorabilia adorn its walls. Sports fans can watch the game on one of the bar's 18 TVs. The menu offers a variety of sandwiches named after Big Ten schools and sports notables—like the Purdue Boilermaker barbecue burger and the Clem Haskins grilled turkey (Clem coached the Gopher basketball team). (*$, (612) 379-1880*)

❹ **Rosen's City Tavern:** With ceiling-mounted TVs tuned to ESPN or local sporting events and vintage photos of old Minneapolis on the walls, Rosen's is a popular game-day destination. Although a crowded house and the roar of multiple TVs can make Rosen's loud on game days, the high-backed booths away from the bar provide a bit of a noise break. The menu sports some huge burgers, salads, and platters of pasta or stir fry. (*$, (612) 338-1926, mplswarehousedistrict.com*) ❺ **Joe Senser's Sports Grill:** One of three sports bars owned by former Viking and 1981 Pro Bowl tight end Joe Senser, this was built with the sports lover in mind. ESPN and *Sports Illustrated* have ranked Joe Senser's one of the top 20 sports bars in America. The walls are plastered with a mix of neon beer signs, autographed jerseys and photos, and large HDTVs. In fact, these giant screens wrap around the entire room. Joe's offers a pretty decent menu, with some Thai, Southwest, salads, appetizers, pasta, sandwiches, and steaks. (*$, (651) 631-1781, sensers.com*)

RESTAURANTS: ❻ **112 Eatery:** This warm, cozy restaurant provides an eclectic American-based menu influenced by European flavors. You'll find French and

Italian influences, even the occasional Asian nod. Enjoy everything from a fried egg and bacon sandwich to tagliatelle pasta with foie gras. Another plus is that entrées that can be ordered half- or full-sized. This is a small restaurant, so waits can be long. On the other hand, the kitchen stays open until 1 a.m. (*$–$$, (612) 343-7696, 112eatery.com*) ❼ **Corner Table:** Corner Table is designed with budget-conscious diners in mind who want to enjoy French bistro-style food. To that end, the dining room tables are topped with touches like stemless Riedel tumblers, while the white walls are hung with mirrors . . . and the menu offers dishes such as Minnesota beef daube Provençal with roasted shallots and lemon-sage potato gratin, and pan-roasted skate wing with diced vegetables, chorizo, manila clams, and a tarragon butter sauce. They also serve a popular brunch. (*$–$$, (612) 823-0011, cornertablerestaurant.com*) ❽ **Gardens of Salonica:** This restaurant provides a setting of polished blond wood floors, tables, and chairs for diners to enjoy traditional and reimagined Greek dishes. The food here is vibrant, thanks to flavors like lemon, garlic, tomatoes, and olive oil, mixing it up with eggplant, lamb, fish, chicken, and pastas. Try the roasted leg of lamb with Greek seasonings and fresh garlic with oven browned potatoes, or the baked cod in olive oil with wine, tomato, onion, parsley, and garlic. (*$, (612) 378-0611, gardensofsalonica.com*) ❾ **Pop! Restaurant:** The "Pop!" is art. The cheerful dining room at Pop! is painted shades of red, yellow, and blue, and decorated with pop art by Andy Warhol, Keith Haring, and others. The kitchen uses Latin, Italian, and Thai influences to create unique dishes; try the sautéed shrimp and chorizo with saffron tomato broth over cous-cous; or the grilled, molé-rubbed salmon with cumin black beans and fruit salsa. Meanwhile, the kids' menu offers six items including pasta, grilled cheese, and fried whitefish fish sticks priced at $6 or less. Note: If you have eight or more in your group, you can call ahead for reservations; if you have fewer than that, then you have to put your name on the list when you get here. (*$, (612) 788-0455, poprestaurant.com*)

Daytime Fun

❶ Mary Tyler Moore Statue: Okay, so this won't take you long to visit, but it is a popular photo op in town. Mary Richards's famous hat toss in the opening of *The Mary Tyler Moore Show* was filmed on Nicollet Mall in downtown Minneapolis. TV Land, the cable network that airs reruns of the popular show, erected a statue of Mary Tyler Moore in mid-toss in the shopping area, and you'll often find people lining up to have their photo taken with the landmark. Many toss their hats in the air, too, but you probably suspected they would. ❷ Mill City Museum: The flour milling industry here dominated the economy from 1880 until about 1930 and earned Minneapolis the nickname "Mill City." This museum explores the milling history from inside the ruins of the Washburn A Mill, which is a National Historic Landmark. It is also the mill that at its peak of production

ground enough flour to make 12 million loaves of bread in a single day. (*$, (612) 341-7555, millcitymuseum.org*) You can also tour **Mills Ruins Park**. (*minneapolisparks.org/default.asp?PageID=4&parkid=413*) ❸ **Minneapolis Institute of Arts:** The Institute's long history (it was established in 1883) includes the recent renovation and addition of the Michael Graves–designed Target wing that opened last year and added 40 percent more gallery space to the building that first welcomed visitors in 1915. All this space is filled with tens of thousands of examples of art ranging from European masters to Asian artisans, Native Americans to contemporary photographers. (*Free, (888) 642-2787, artsmia.org*) ❹ **Minneapolis Sculpture Garden:** They say the 11-acre park is the largest urban sculpture garden in the country. There are 40 permanent pieces joined by a rotation of temporary exhibits. The Garden is next to the **Walker Art Center** (which is in the midst of expanding, including more green space that will host additional sculptures) and **Loring Park**. The Garden's centerpiece is the instantly memorable *Spoonbridge and Cherry*, an oversized spoon holding a cherry that is a fountain piece at the Garden. (*Free, garden.walkerart.org*)

Nighttime Fun

❶ The Big 10: This is the way college restaurants and bars should be. Long bars and booths with more than 40 years of U of M history etched into them, and lots of college kids have made this a student and alumni favorite in Stadium Village. *City Pages* has named The Big 10 the "Best Place to Take Out of Town Guests" so don't be surprised to see visiting fans here. The menu features wings, subs, and the like. There're always drink specials at the bar, too. (*$, (612) 378-0467, big10restaurant.com/StadiumVillage.htm*) **❷ First Avenue:** This curved building downtown was originally a bus station, but for nearly 40 years it's been the place for live music in Minneapolis. Everyone from Culture Club to REM, the Kinks to Sonic Youth has played here. But First Avenue's most famous act is Prince, who in the 1980s made this his regular venue to work out new music and wow crowds. It was also the set for *Purple Rain*. Today national acts still play First Avenue as do regional and local bands. (*$, (612) 332-1775, first-avenue.com*) **❸ Infinity:** This is the one of the city's hip, sleek, stylish nightclubs. According to many publications, it's the best, too. *Conde Nast* named it one of the top 30 nightclubs in the world, and its interior has won style awards to go with the kudos on atmosphere. Dress to be seen, and to dance—the DJs here are about as well-known as the club. (*$–$$, (612) 312-1123, infinitylounge.com*) **❹ Minnesota Zephyr:** The Minnesota Zephyr Railroad was built more than 135 years ago and this dinner train—with five unique,

restored dining cars—re-creates the days of the rails in the 1940s. The train travels for 3 ½ hours along the river, streams, and bluffs of the St. Croix River Valley. The menus offer dishes ranging from salmon to prime rib to Rock Game Hen. Your meal will also be serenaded by The Zephyr Cabaret, entertainers in period dress singing the hits of the 1940s and 1950s to complete the historical mood. (*$$$, (800) 992-6100, minnesotazephyr.com*) ❺ **Warehouse District:** This historic district is home to a thriving nightlife. From the three levels of **Club 3** (which include dancing, pool and sports, and a café), to "interactive live bands" at **The Lodge Bar**, to the high-tech **Escape Ultra Lounge**, you'll find something to do late into the night. The Warehouse District also has restaurants and shopping. (*$–$$, mplswarehouse.com*)

Shopping

❶ **Mall of America:** It's one of the largest shopping malls in the world (4.2 million square feet), and it's the most visited on the planet (more than 40 million each year). Inside there are 2.5 million square feet of shopping, an indoor amusement park, a campus for the National American University, a bunch of restaurants, and more—even a wedding chapel. While this is a shopping mall, it's also a must-see attraction. Plan to spend a few hours. (*(952) 883-8800, mallofamerica.com*) ❷ **Nicollet Mall:** This upscale shopping area is in downtown Minneapolis and near the Hubert H. Humphrey Metrodome. You'll find a number of national and regional shops including big boys such as **Macy's** and **Neiman Marcus**. ❸ **University of Minnesota Bookstores:** If you need Gopher gear, you're not going to find a place with more of it. In addition to apparel and gifts, they have everything from tailgating gear to balloon bouquets, and they have gear for a number of U of M sports (Minnesota volleyball shot glass, anyone?). The main store is on campus in the Coffman Union on Washington Ave., SE (*(612) 625-6000, bookstore.umn.edu/shopping/ mwear.html*)

NORTHWESTERN

Northwestern University: 13,405 students
Evanston, IL: pop. 74,239
Ryan Field: seats 47,130
Colors: Purple and White
Nickname: Wildcats
Mascot: Willie
Phone: (847) 491-CATS

Overnight RV parking available at Campus Lot 2, $30 a day. RVs can arrive 6 p.m. Friday. No parking available around Ryan Field, make use of numerous city and campus lots. Tailgating starts 7 a.m. Saturday, and continues throughout game. The only real restriction is no glass containers. Otherwise, use common sense. RVs leave by 12 noon Sunday.

Shuttle Info: Free shuttle service provided for anyone parking in an on-campus lot, starting 2 hours before game, running until 1 hour postgame.

Wildcats Media Partner: 720-AM WGN

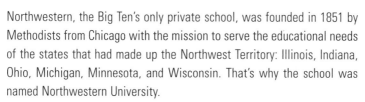

Northwestern, the Big Ten's only private school, was founded in 1851 by Methodists from Chicago with the mission to serve the educational needs of the states that had made up the Northwest Territory: Illinois, Indiana, Ohio, Michigan, Minnesota, and Wisconsin. That's why the school was named Northwestern University.

In 1873 the Evanston College for Ladies merged with Northwestern, which made famed women's suffragist Frances Willard the school's first Dean of Women. Her efforts are credited as instrumental in passage of the 19th Amendment to the U.S. Constitution, which gave women the right to vote. (Her other passion was the fight against alcohol, and her efforts there are given the same credit for passing the 18th Amendment, which ushered in Prohibition.)

In the 1930s another merger almost eliminated Northwestern.

The presidents of Northwestern and its academic neighbor and rival the University of Chicago proposed merging the schools to create the Universities of Chicago. They felt the combined school would be a world leader and was vital for the survival of both institutions. Northwestern's board didn't see it that way and killed the plan.

As a result, the university still stands and has become one of the nation's most highly respected academic and research institutions. It is also one of the most selective universities in the nation—ranked 14th in that category by *U.S. News and World Report.*

The same cannot be said for its football program.

The Northwestern football program began between 1876 and 1882, depending on which source you believe. What's not in question is that the success of the program during the next 100 or so years has been scattered at best.

The Wildcats can point to successes from 1903 to 1936, including 5 Big Ten titles, but not much else positive happened until the 1990s.

During that dry spell the Wildcats had a 34-game losing streak, an NCAA record. When the record was set by a 61–14 loss to Michigan State, Wildcat fans took to the field chanting, "We're the worst!" At least they had a sense of humor about it.

In 1992 coach Gary Barnett came to Evanston, and by 1995 he had Wildcats fans chanting a different message with a Big Ten championship and a berth in the Rose Bowl. The next year Northwestern repeated as conference champs and played in the Citrus Bowl.

While there has been one conference championship since (2000) and a couple of bowl games, the Wildcats most often find themselves in the middle of the Big Ten pack.

School Mascot

Originally, Northwestern's teams went by the names The Purple and The Fighting Methodists. But a *Chicago Tribune* writer changed that forever. When reporting about how the team played in a 1924 game, he wrote, "Football players had not come down from Evanston; Wildcats would be a name better suited."

The university liked the name so much they adopted it as the official school nickname just a few months later.

But before they were the Wildcats, a live bear cub named Furpaw was the team mascot. Before each game in 1923 the caged bear was taken to the field to greet fans. But 1923 was a losing season, and the team decided their bad luck was Furpaw's fault. The bear was banned from campus.

Willie the Wildcat is the mascot now. He was the brainchild of the athletic department and an ad agency in 1933. You can thank the Alpha Delta fraternity for bringing Willie to life. Fraternity members dressed up in the first Willie outfit in

Go U Northwestern!

Break right through that.

With our colors flying, we will cheer you all
the time. U rah! Rah!

Go U Northwestern!

Fight for victory!

Spread far the fame of our fair name.

Go Northwestern, win that game!

Go Northwestern, go!

Go Northwestern, go!

Hit 'em high! Hit 'em low!

Go Northwestern, go!

Go U Northwestern!

Break right through that.

With our colors flying, we will cheer you all
the time. U rah! Rah!

Go U Northwestern!

Fight for victory!

Spread far the fame of our fair name.

Go Northwestern, win that game!

1947 for the school's Homecoming parade.

Game-Day Traditions

Jingling the Keys

There are several schools around the country where it is tradition for students to pull out their car keys and jingle them at certain times of the game. At some schools it's a quiet cheer for the offense—showing support without getting so loud to make it hard for the team to hear the quarterback. Not at Northwestern.

Here it's more of a taunt. The Wildcats have much more often than not been on the losing side of the scoreboard, and the keys are meant as an arrogant status symbol to opponents saying: "You might win the game, but before long your school's graduates will be parking our cars."

Push-ups and the Wildcat Claw

After every touchdown Willie the Wildcat drops to the turf and does a push-up for each point Northwestern has on the scoreboard. Lots of mascots around the country do that. But at Northwestern the student section joins in. Usually this takes place by students in the stands lifting fellow students up and down while counting off the number of points the Wildcats have scored.

This exercise is often accompanied by students making a claw with their hands, extending them into the air, and screaming like a Wildcat. The hand sign happens without the scoring, too, of course.

Visiting Northwestern

Northwestern sits along the shore of Lake Michigan in Evanston, just 20 miles north of Chicago. While there are things to do in town, many go into Chicago to eat, shop, and enjoy the nightlife. That's one reason why many of the places I talk about in this chapter are in the Windy City. Evanston is named for John Evans, one of Northwestern's founders. It is also the place where Tinkertoys were created.

Where to Stay

❶ The Homestead: Built in 1927, it's been family owned and operated for more than 75 years. The Homestead's 90-room, Colonial-style inn is two blocks from Northwestern and Lake Michigan, on a quiet residential street. Conditions are clean and comfortable, but a bit old-fashioned—guestrooms have either one queen or two twin beds, and window units. Most rooms still have their original 1927 fixtures and are bright, airy, and rather large. Rates run $130–$140. Studios and one- or two-bedroom apartments are available for extended stays. (*(847) 475-3300, thehomestead.net*) **❷ Hotel Allegro:** Located in Chicago's theater district, this Art Deco–designed hotel has bright colors and a hip, club-like atmosphere. In your room you'll find a flat-screen TV, sound system, and a fully stocked minibar, alongside the usual amenities. Rooms run $129–$229. (*(866) 672-6143, allegrochicago.com*) **❸ Hotel Orrington:** It's not cheap, but you're only a little more than a mile and a half from Ryan Stadium here. The Orrington was recently renovated, and the rooms are decorated to look like a boutique hotel, with warm colors and stylish furnishings. Guestrooms also have free high-speed Internet access. Bathrooms are on the small side, as are the closets, but you do get Aveda toiletries in the bath. The hotel's third floor is dog-friendly. Rates during football season run $249–$279 for a room, $379–$1,400 for a suite. Prices vary according to occupancy, so call ahead. (*(888) 677-4648, hotelorrington.com*) ❹ **Janet's Place Bed & Breakfast:** Janet's is the only B&B in Evanston proper. There are five guestrooms here, two with private baths. Built in 1917, the inn is located in Evanston's Lakefront District and close to the beach, parks, and Main Street shopping. The home's second floor includes a sun room, and the house has WiFi available throughout. (*(847) 328-8966, janetspl.com*) ❺ **Palmer House:** This historic Chicago landmark was destroyed in the 1871 fire and was rebuilt more opulently than before. The hand-painted ceiling in the lobby is simply spectacular. Of course, the hotel's been renovated a couple more times since the late 1800s, and rooms offer all the basic amenities. There's also a fitness center. I'm breaking my chain hotel rule a bit by including the Palmer House, since it's now owned by Hilton, but the history and architecture are worth the exception. Rooms will cost you $179–$234. (*(800) 445-8667, hilton.com—search for Chicago, IL*) ❻ **Paul Wolff Campground:** Located in Elgin, it's probably the closest RV park to Evanston. Luckily, it's also pretty nice. There are 48 RV sites with water and electric hookups. The paved

sites are clean and generously sized, in a pleasant setting—the campground is part of Burnidge Forest Preserve. Like most state or county park campgrounds, there are no cable, phone, or Internet connections; activities center on the preserve's natural attractions. A dump station is available. Note that the place shuts down for the season on Halloween night. Sites are $15. (*(630) 444-1200, co.kane.il.us/Forest/fp/burnidge_paulwolff.htm*)

❼ The Wheeler Mansion: This 1870 historical landmark is one of the last of the stately mansions that survived the Great Chicago Fire. Although it is a B&B, it acts more like a boutique hotel. The house has seven guestrooms, two junior suites, and two full suites, all with private baths. Suites have fireplaces. Rooms run $230–$285; suites cost up to $365. (*(312) 945-2020, wheelermansion.com*) ❽ **Windy City Beach & Camping Resort:** Situated between Chicago and the Chicagoland Speedway, this park offers 100 full hookup sites, a small lake with a beach, fishing, paddle boats, and a snack shop. Daily rates run $32–$34. Cabins available. (*(708) 720-0030, windycitycampground.com*)

Where to Eat

TAILGATER SUPPLIES: ❶ **Evanston Farmers' Market:** For more than 28 years, the Evanston Farmers' Market has been a crowd-pleaser with more than 30 vendors selling produce, meat, flowers, cheese, and bakery items. The market is open every Saturday until November at the intersection of University Place and Oak Avenue. (*(847) 866-2936*)

SPORTS BARS: There aren't any traditional sports bars in Evanston, so you'll want to head into Chicago for that experience. If you want to hang out around campus, **The Keg of Evanston** and the **Celtic Knot Public House** are good bets, but they aren't sports bars. That's why they're in the Nighttime Fun section.

❷ **ESPN Zone:** The 16-foot HDTV big screen tells you this is a serious sports bar. Then again, it's the branded bar from a serious sports network. In addition to watching games, you can play them, including Madden NFL Football on a 15-foot screen and an interactive Power Pitcher, where you can try to strike out Jeter, Pujols, and Ramirez. (*$, (312) 644-3776, espnzone.com/Chicago*)

❸ **Murphy's Bleachers:** The place opened in 1930 as Ernie's Bleachers, became Ray's Bleachers in 1965 (remember the Bleacher Bums?), and changed to Murphy's Bleachers when Jim Murphy bought it in 1980. It sits across the street from Wrigley Field and is a Chicago institution. It's also been named "Chicago's Best Bar" by *AOL CityGuide*. The food is mostly burgers and sandwiches. (*$, (773) 281-5356, murphysbleachers.com*)

RESTAURANTS: ❹ **Chef's Station:** This European-style bistro has put a lot of thought into its menu and carefully selected wine list. The menu changes

weekly, listing updated versions of American classics like center-cut New York Steak, with European dishes like pan-seared skate wing. The restaurant has lots of funky touches that make eating here fun—check out the sky-blue director's chairs at dining tables, and recycled jean pockets serving as silverware holders. You'll find it under the Davis Street Metro Station. (*$$, (847) 570-9821, chefs-station.com*) ❺ **Gino's East of Chicago:** This is one of the places that helped make Chicago-style, deep-dish pizza famous. The Chicago landmark opened in 1966, and there have been lines for their pies ever since. You can order thin-crust pizza, too, but why would you? (*$, (312) 943-1124, ginoseast.com*) ❻ **Harry Caray's Restaurant:** Named for the late Hall of Fame baseball announcer, this Chicago favorite is housed in the last example of 19th-century Dutch Renaissance architecture left in Chicago (it was built in 1895). But it's Harry Caray's steaks, wine, and bar scene that's won awards. As you'd expect, there's memorabilia from the Chicago legend's broadcast career and a gift shop where you can buy "Holy Cow" merchandise. (*$$, (312) 828-0966, harrycarays.com*) ❼ **Lulu's Dim Sum & Then Sum:** A favorite with locals and university students alike, this spot can get busy during peak hours. Big paper lanterns lend atmosphere, along with a mural above the counter. A Buddha stands smiling in the corner. The full menu divides into three sections: fun dim sum bites, salads and noodle soups, and stir-fry or noodle plates. Try Lulu's bento box for a great sampling of tastes or the large teriyaki salad. (*$, (847) 869-4343, lulusdimsum.com*) ❽ **Mike Ditka's Chicago:** He won a Super Bowl here coaching the Bears (he also won one in Dallas as a player), and "Da' Coach" is still as loved today in the Windy City as after that 1985 season. So is his food. The menu covers steaks to chops, fish to pasta. And the answer to your question is, yes, he does show up now and then to mingle and sign autographs. (*$–$$, (312) 587-8989, mikeditkaschicago.com*)

❾ **Wolfgang Puck Grand Café:** It's Puck's LA style in The Land of Lincoln. Walls of windows with yellow, green, and purple panels keep things sunny, while funky tiles, urns, and light fixtures add charm to this bustling restaurant. The menu is an extensive selection of entrées, including Puck's signature wood-fired pizzas. The wine list has a focus on American wines. (*$–$$, (847) 869-9653, wolfgangpuck. com/rest/cafe/evanston.php*)

Daytime Fun

❶ **Art Institute of Chicago:** This is where you can see Grant Wood's *American Gothic*, Edward Hopper's *Nighthawks*, Pablo Picasso's *The Old Guitarist*, and Georges Seurat's *A Sunday Afternoon on La Grande Jatte–1884*. The Art Institute is considered one of the best museums in the world. In addition to the art inside, you'll probably recognize the two lion statues flanking the museum's main entrance outside; they've been there since 1893. (*$$, (312) 443-3600, artic.edu*) ❷ **Chicago Museum Campus:** The lakefront park covers 57 acres. Actually, it's a series of public parks and gardens that connect the city's three most prominent museums, which include: **Adler Planetarium & Astronomy Museum:** The first public planetarium in the western hemisphere (opened in 1930) is still showing the night sky—but with much better equipment and exhibits. One of those exhibits is a space-flight simulator. (*$$, (312) 922-STAR, adlerplanetarium.org*) **Field Museum of Natural History:** His department store may be gone (Marshall Field's is now Macy's), but the museum named for benefactor Marshall Field is still wowing them with exhibits illustrating art, archaeology, science, and history from around the world. You can see the world's largest Tyrannosaurus rex and King Tut here. (*$$, (312) 922-9410, fieldmuseum.org*) **John G. Shedd Aquarium:** There isn't a larger aquarium in the world (a title it's owned since its 1930 opening). The Shedd has exhibits featuring fish and animals from around the world. Some are in pools that appear to blend into Lake Michigan. (*$$, (312) 939-2426, sheddaquarium.org*) ❸ **The Frances Willard House:** Frances Willard was Northwestern's first Dean of Women. She was also one of the most prominent social reformers in 19th-century America as president of the Women's Christian Temperance Union. The museum's exhibits chronicle Willard's life and work as one of the nation's most prominent women of her time. (*$, (847) 328-7500, franceswillardhouse.org*) ❹ **Navy Pier:** Built in 1916, it was originally a commercial shipping pier; now it's an entertainment destination. The easiest way to recognize it is by its most famous attraction: a 150-foot-high Ferris wheel, which was built in 1893 for the city's World Columbian Exposition and later moved here. Other attractions include an IMAX theater, miniature golf, the **Children's Museum**, a carousel, shopping, and restaurants. (*$, (312) 595-7437, navypier.com*) ❺ **Sears Tower Skydeck:** The Skydeck in this 110-story building (once the world's tallest) has

exhibits, interactive kiosks, and telescopes. And a great view. On a clear day you can see Illinois, Michigan, Indiana, and Wisconsin from here. In case you're wondering, that's more than 50 miles any direction. (*$–$$, 233 S. Wacker Dr., Chicago, (312) 875-9696, the-skydeck.com*)

Nighttime Fun

❶ **Buddy Guy's Legends:** Legends is one of the top blues clubs in America. That's fitting for a guy who is a musical legend himself (and in the Rock and Roll Hall of Fame). And when you're a legend, other legends want to play your venue. That's why folks such as Eric Clapton, Stevie Ray Vaughn, and ZZ Top have played the Chicago club. Most nights, of course, feature local, regional, and touring acts. You can always get a taste of the big time, though, from all of the memorabilia hanging on the walls. (*$–$$, (312) 427-0333, buddyguys.com*)

❷ **The Celtic Knot Public House:** This traditional Irish Pub is a popular spot for Northwestern students and Evanston locals alike. The menu keeps the traditional feel with dishes such as fish and chips and Shepherd's Pie, but also has some more modern touches such as the Pecan Crusted Salmon. Plenty of dark, rich beers on tap, too. The Knot has live music many nights. (*$, (847) 864-*

1679, celticknotpub.com) ❸ **The Cotton Club:** The original is in Harlem, but the Chicago location is a popular spot for live music. The Cab Calloway room features contemporary jazz and blues combos. DJs spin hip-hop and urban contemporary in the rear Gray Room. And if you're wondering, the name isn't about what your shirt's made of; it comes from a definition of cotton, meaning "to make friends." (*$, (312) 341-9787, cottonclubchicago.com*) ❹ **The Keg of Evanston:** This hangout is close to Northwestern and very popular with students who go there. It's part-pub, part-restaurant, with a full menu. But it's The Keg's two bars, game room, and party atmosphere that packs them in. Right after work and for dinner, the crowd sometimes skews a bit older, but the evening and night is all about the college kids. (*$, (847) 869-9987*) ❺ **Sound-Bar:** This place is big—20,000 square feet and multilevel—and one of Chicago's hippest dance clubs. With several bars and lounges and a 4,000-square-foot dance floor, you'll find a spot to enjoy yourself. (*$–$$, (312) 787-4480, sound-bar.com*)

Shopping

❶ **The Magnificent Mile:** Everything you need is along Chicago's Michigan Avenue. So are things you don't need but want anyway. Bounded by Oak Street

on the north and the Chicago River to the south, you'll find more than 450 retail stores, including **Neiman Marcus**, **Saks Fifth Avenue**, and **Bloomingdale's**. There are also scores of smaller shops and boutiques, restaurants, and clubs. (*themagnificentmile.com*) ❷ **Norris Center Bookstore:** If you enter the Norris University Center on the ground level, you'll find the Norris Center Bookstore and a sea of purple merchandise. There's stuff for you and your kids to wear and to stick on your car. Most anything you need with a Wildcat on it is here. So is that transport phenomena chemical engineering textbook you've been wanting to curl up with. (*(847) 491-3990, northwestern.bkstore.com*)

OHIO STATE

The Ohio State University: 54,989 students
Columbus, OH: pop. 711,470
Ohio Stadium: seats 101,568
Colors: Scarlet and Gray
Nickname: Buckeyes
Mascot: Brutus Buckeye
Phone: (614) 292-2624

Football parking varies, depending on which game and whether other varsity sports (basketball) are also playing. In general, RVs arrive Friday before the game, sometimes as early as 7 a.m., and park in Buckeye Lots across from Jesse Owens Memorial Stadium. RV is parking first-come, first-served, $30 to $50 for weekend, depending on game. Cars park for $10. Open container laws in effect; be discreet. Grills only allowed on surfaced lots.

Shuttle Info: Free shuttle service for fans parked on West Campus.

Buckeyes Media Partners: 1460-AM and 97.1-FM WBNS

When the state was deciding what school would be its land-grant university (as a part of the Morrill Act of 1862), Ohio's two existing public universities brought in their big guns who pled with the state legislature to "pick me." But Governor Rutherford B. Hayes—who would later serve as president of the United States—had other ideas and convinced the legislature to pick neither Ohio University nor Miami University and, instead, create a new school located near the legislature in Columbus.

That school was founded in 1870 as The Ohio Agricultural and Mechanical College. The school's early years were tough as it fought for resources against Ohio and Miami universities who were bitter about the land-grant decision. The school also had to fend off hostility from the state's

agricultural interests who were opposed to the school's efforts to broaden its instructional programs beyond agriculture and mechanical instruction.

After returning to Ohio from the White House in 1881, Rutherford B. Hayes took strong interest in the school and used his significant political clout to ensure the university's funding and stature. He served on the Board of Trustees and often acted as if he were the university's president. His support helped the school, later renamed The Ohio State University, become Ohio's flagship university.

It has since grown into one of the largest universities in America with more than 50,000 students and is consistently ranked among the best public universities in the country.

Its football team is also consistently ranked as one of the best in the country. The Buckeyes have racked up 33 conference championships and 5 national titles. But an incident in 1901 almost prevented it all from happening.

Football first found its way to campus in 1890. Most credit George Cole, a student at the time, with organizing the first team. He recruited a coach, and the Buckeyes played their first game at Ohio Wesleyan University on May 3, 1890. OSU won.

During the next 9 years the team had several coaches and amassed a record of

31-39-2. But in 1899 the university hired a new coach who used professional coaching tactics and turned the program around, going undefeated that year and 8-1-1 the next.

But in 1901 Buckeyes center John Sigrist died from injuries suffered in a game against Western Reserve. Incidents like this were not unheard of in collegiate football at the time, and several schools had shut down their football programs as a result. The faculty at Ohio State wanted to be one of those schools and passed a resolution to shutter the football program. The athletic department left it up to the team to decide what it wanted to do. The team fought the resolution, and the proposal was narrowly defeated.

Ohio State solidified its place on the national stage in 1942 when it won its first national championship, despite fielding a team that had lost most of its starters to military service. The legendary Paul Brown coached that team. He had been hired the year before after the entire OSU coaching staff resigned following a 4-4 season. Brown had yet to become legendary or known as the "father of the modern offense," but he came to OSU from an Ohio high school where his team had outscored its opponents 477-6 on its way to a sixth state title. After leaving Ohio

State, Brown went on to coach the Cleveland Browns and Cincinnati Bengals, winning several professional championships.

A handful of coaches succeeded Brown until 1951 when Woody Hayes was hired. He wasn't the school's first choice. Missouri head coach Don Fourot was. In fact, Fourot had accepted the job, but changed his mind a couple of days later. Enter Woody.

Hayes received criticism at first for his aggressive style and personality, and for not winning more games. He had a philosophy of football that was conservative and tough, and no amount of criticism was going to change his style of coaching or of play. In the end, it worked for him.

Hayes coached for 28 seasons and left OSU with a record of 205-61-10. He won 13 Big Ten titles, 3 national championships (1954, 1957, and 1968), and coached 4 Heisman Trophy winners, including 2-time winner Archie Griffin.

But in the end Hayes's temper caught up with him. He was fired after punching a Clemson player in the throat after the player had intercepted a pass near the end of a game. ESPN calls his actions "the most unsportsmanlike behavior of all time."

Ohio State won its fifth national championship in 2002 under coach Jim Tressel.

School Mascot

First, let's get the basics out of the way. A buckeye is a small, dark brown nut accented with a small tan patch. It comes from the buckeye tree, which is Ohio's state tree. Legend has it the buckeye resembles a deer's eye, and carrying one with you will bring you good luck. Ohio officially has been the Buckeye State since 1950, although folks called it that for many years prior.

The state nickname became the school nickname thanks, in part, to OSU student Ray Bourhis who convinced the athletic department it needed a mascot. It was 1965, and many other schools were incorporating mascots into their programs, most by using live animals. OSU first considered that, but a buck deer was the only animal that would have made sense and, well, they don't hang out on sidelines all that well.

So a buckeye nut was created from papier-mâché and worn by a student who roamed the sidelines and stands. A campus-wide naming contest conceived the name Brutus Buckeye.

Papier-mâché turned out not to be the best material for a big nut head, and it was quickly replaced with fiberglass. It has since been updated to look more

current and be more comfortable for the handful of students who trade-off wearing the costume each year.

The Buckeye Leaves on the players' helmets are the legacy of coach Woody Hayes who redesigned the team's look in 1968. The now-famous Buckeye Leaves stickers are awarded for big plays and consistency on the field. Many OSU sports have adopted the Buckeye Leaves.

Game-Day Traditions
Buckeye Grove

The small forest near the southwest corner of the stadium, near Morrill Tower, is Buckeye Grove and where fans go to remember Buckeye greats of the past. Each tree planted here honors an OSU player named first team All-American. Trees honoring new All-Americans are planted during ceremonies before the Spring Game each year. The first OSU All-American was named in 1914, and now more than 125 trees stand in the Grove.

Michigan Week

The Ohio State–Michigan rivalry is one of the most heated and anticipated in football. ESPN calls it the best in the country. The faithful call it simply, "The

Game." If you happen to be in Columbus for Michigan Week, you'll find a city that starts the pregame and tailgating on Thursday. The last of the fans clean up and move out on Sunday.

Thursday night the unofficial traditions kick-off with the **Mirror Lake Jump**. Scores of students jump into this small lake between Pomerence Hall and The Oval to kickoff the celebrations. Keep in mind this game is always near the end of the season, and it's Ohio, so it's usually cold. Often, very cold.

The Tunnel of Pride falls on the official side of traditions and takes place at Ohio Stadium. At Michigan home games, since 1994, former players have lined up and formed a tunnel through which the current players run as they take the field. The school uses this tradition not just as motivation before a big game, but as a way to connect former players with current ones, which otherwise might not happen.

Victory Bell

Hanging 150 feet above the ground in the southeast tower of Ohio Stadium is a 2,420 pound gift from the Classes of 1943–1945. The Victory Bell, as it's called, initially rang every now and then. One of those "now" times was after OSU's win against California in 1954; that ringing began a tradition of Alpha Phi Omega members ringing the bell after every Ohio State victory. They say the bell can be heard up to 5 miles away, and only after one game was the bell silent.

After a 1965 win over Iowa students ran up the tower to ring the bell but found someone had stolen the bell's clapper. They hit the bell with a hammer to try and "ring" it, but they were the only ones who heard anything. The missing clapper turned up the following week hanging from a statue on campus, and the bell was repaired. No one knows who the pranksters were.

Visiting Ohio State

Columbus was founded as a compromise. In the early 1800s Ohio's state capital was moved from Chillicothe to Zanesville. Then from Zanesville to Chillicothe. The legislature decided a city near the center of the state would be a good compromise for the state capital, and land speculators made an offer. The legislature liked the plan—a town was born and named for Christopher Columbus. Today Columbus is the 15th largest city in the country, and in addition to education, insurance is a major industry here. The city is home to five major insurance companies including Nationwide Insurance.

Where to Stay

❶ 50 Lincoln Inn: This restored 19th-century townhouse has eight guestrooms, each decorated in the style of a different artist. Rooms have queen-size beds, private baths, voice mail, data ports, and cable TV. Downstairs, a gallery displays works by local artists, rotating every 2 months. Rooms are $119. (*(800) 827-4203, columbus-bed-breakfast.com*) ❷ **Alton RV Park:** It's in the heart of Columbus, just a hop and a skip from campus (depending on how far you can hop and skip). There are 35 graveled sites here with full hookups. Most sites also have phone hookups and WiFi, and there's a dump station. This is strictly a well-kept stopover park, perfect for football fans in town for the game. And a lot of fans roll into town for games, so be sure to call ahead for reservations. Sites are $25–$30. (*(614) 878-9127, altonrvpark.com*) ❸ **Blackwell Hotel & Conference Center:** This upscale hotel sits right on campus and is decorated in modified Mission style with soft tones and wood. Guestrooms have extras like leather chairs, pillow-top mattresses, and plush bathrobes. Access to the 24-hour fitness center is free, and there's a good restaurant on-site. During football season rooms run $249–$499 with a two-night minimum stay. They start taking reservations for football season in January, and they sell out quickly, so get those fingers dialing. (*(866) 247-4003, theblackwell.com*) ❹ **Harrison House**

Bed & Breakfast: It's easy to imagine yourself in another time, sitting in a wicker chair on the front porch of this turquoise-and-cream 1890 Queen Anne. This B&B offers four large, attractive bedrooms with private baths, data ports, and cable TV. Rooms are individually styled but maintain an overall scheme that's historically accurate. Previous guests rave about the service and the candlelit breakfast. Rooms cost $119. (*(800) 827-4203, columbus-bed-breakfast.com*) ❺ **House of the Seven Goebels:** I don't know what the Seven Goebels are, but I do know this is a reproduction of a 1780 Connecticut River Valley farmhouse sitting on two landscaped acres. It was built with historically accurate materials and methods, like square nails, hand-split Shaker roofing, and handmade doors with wooden latches. It offers two guestrooms, the Red Room and Blue Room, each with a fireplace. The first has an attached private bath; the second has a larger, unattached private bath. The whole house is furnished in a manner too luxurious to call Colonial, but too understated to call Victorian. Rooms run $100 for two people, $85 for one person. (*(614) 761-9595, bbhost.com/7goebels*) ❻ **Lofts Hotel:** This unique property was converted from an 1882 warehouse to a 44-guestroom hotel. Its large, loftlike rooms have exposed bricks and beams, arched doorways, and floor-to-ceiling windows. The atmosphere is a mix of Ralph Lauren and IKEA with warm tones, clean lines, and natural materials. You'll enjoy nice touches here like Fretté terry robes and bed linens, and Aveda bath products. Rooms run $189–$289 during football season. (*(800) 73LOFTS, 55lofts.com*)

Where to Eat

TAILGATER SUPPLIES: ❶ **North Market:** This is more upscale than your typical farmers' market. It's also the last public market in Central Ohio, open since 1876. Outside is the farmers' market area, open every Saturday until early November, with produce, plants and flowers, and more. Inside, you'll find meats, dairy, eggs, baked goods, and multicultural and alternative products year-round at 32 individually owned stands. (*(614) 463-9664, northmarket.com*)

SPORTS BARS: ❷ **The Buckeye Hall of Fame Café:** You have to see it to believe it. This restaurant-bar-museum has more than 50,000 square feet of space dedicated to OSU. There's a trophy hall and all manner of Buckeye paraphernalia, photos, and memorabilia. It's like a Planet Hollywood (Planet Buckeye?) for fans who bleed scarlet and gray. There are even stars on the floor with names of former Buckeyes. The casual Arena Room has big-screen TVs for

watching the game while noshing on burgers and wings. Upscale selections like prime rib and filet mignon can be had in the dressier Trophy Room. *($–$$, (614) 291-2233, buckeyehallof fame.com)* ❸ **Eddie George's Grille 27:** It's Eddie George's place, and the OSU star and Heisman Trophy winner drops by about once a month. With 41 plasma-screen TVs, you won't miss the game no matter where you sit. The interior's design is sleek, with an oval bar and a palette of scarlet, gray, and cream. There's some Eddie

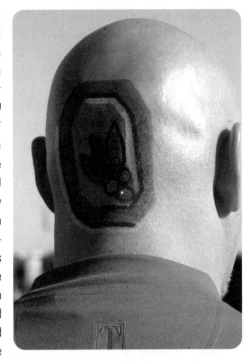

George memorabilia on the walls, but not as much as you'd expect. The menu ranges from classic pub fare to upscale options like seared peppercorn-crusted Ahi tuna with couscous. In honor of Eddie's college and NFL jersey number (all but 1 year of his pro career was with the Houston Oilers/Tennessee Titans), there are 27 wines, 27 beers, 27 specialty drinks, and a 27-ounce porterhouse steak. *($, (614) 421-2727)* ❹ **Library Bar:** An icon all its own on OSU's High Street, this bar has five large TVs for game watching and two floors full of college bar fun. Grab a seat on the ground floor to hang with a lively crowd and play pool, foosball, shuffle bowling, and the Mega Touch or Cruisin' World games. Head to the basement for darts, some neat vintage pinball, and a more laid-back crowd. *($, (614) 299-3245, librarybar.com)* ❺ **Varsity Club:** One look at this place tells you you're in Buckeye country. The exterior is scarlet and gray, and their menu and decorations (even the jukebox) celebrate Ohio State sports. If you're planning to watch the OSU game here, come early or you won't get in—

like several hours early. Most Fridays there's live music. During off-season, the crowd is thinner, but fans still watch the game dú jour on one of the Varsity's many TVs. The menu includes dishes from burgers to spaghetti to salads. (*$*, *(614) 299-6269*)

RESTAURANTS: ❻ **Dragonfly Neo V Cuisine:** This award-winning gourmet vegetarian restaurant uses local organic ingredients, some sprouting from a garden outside the kitchen door. The four-course menu changes daily, but expect dishes such as wild walnut ricotta ravioli and sun-dried tomato risotto. Dragonfly also serves a very creative list of cocktails using herbal infusions. The interior, done in soothing colors with glass art and oil paintings, manages to be both elegant and eclectic. (*$, (614) 298-9986, dragonflyneov.com*) ❼ **The Refectory:** With its stained glass windows and wooden beams, the dining room still has a reverent atmosphere for this church-turned-restaurant, perfect for heavenly service and classic French food. The menu provides starters such as roast goat cheese with baby beets, and pheasant and foie gras terrine. Main dishes include venison loin with a plum Bordelaise sauce, and pan-seared Ohio rainbow trout with mushroom duxelle. Dinners here are leisurely, but

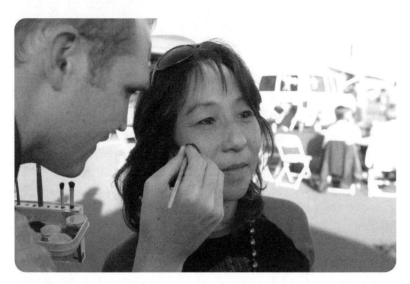

reservations are suggested. You may also find the church's former pastor at the table next to you; he still comes by to celebrate special occasions. (*$$, (614) 451-9774, refectory.com*) ❽ **Starliner Diner:** This Cuban-American diner is a treat for your eyes, as well as your mouth. The interior is covered with fantastical murals, whimsical clocks, statues, and signs. The breakfast menu has chorizo omelets, breakfast burritos, and banana pancakes; the lunch menu features Cuban sandwiches, burritos, burgers, and more; the dinner menu has adobo pork loin, Cuban-style roast chicken, and accompaniments like plantains, black beans, and Cuban bread. (*$, (614) 529-1198, starlinerdiner.com*) ❾ **Z Cucina:** Often the best dishes at this open, airy restaurant aren't listed on the menu. They're the pasta, fish, or other entrée of the day, such as the chef's Mediterranean seafood stew featuring rock shrimp, fish, and mussels in a fennel-saffron broth. That doesn't mean the menu isn't good—it is. The duck breast Piedmontese with mascarpone polenta and cranberry mustard is a customer favorite. (*$–$$, (614) 486-9200, zcucina.com*)

Daytime Fun

❶ **Columbus Zoo and Aquarium:** This is the place where Jack Hanna works. You know, the guy who brings the animals that climb all over Leno and

Letterman. He's Director Emeritus of the zoo, which has 6,000 animals from across the globe. The new Asia Quest exhibit area simulates a Himalayan village with sun bears, red pandas, and a Siberian tiger. There are animal shows and activities for kids, too. (*$–$$, (614) 645-3550, columbuszoo.org*) ❷ **Field of Corn:** Don't try harvesting this corn; it's as tall as you are (maybe taller) and made of concrete. No, it isn't a joke (although many Dublin taxpayers think differently). It's a public art project city leaders in the Columbus suburb of Dublin commissioned in 1994. The 109 concrete ears stand on the Sam and Eulalia Frantz Park—the same land that Sam Frantz used to farm corn and develop several mutant strains that you eat today. He worked with OSU on hybridization projects, and the public art display was designed to commemorate his work. If you're wondering—or just want to win a bet—the type of corn "growing" here is a double-crossed hybrid called Corn Belt Dent Corn. (*Free, dublinvisit.org/visitors/attractions/art_in_public.htm*) ❸ **Franklin Park Conservatory:** Built in 1895, the Conservatory is on the National Register of Historic Places and houses more than 400 plant species in collections ranging from Himalayan Mountains to Tropical Rainforest to Desert. It is also the only botanical garden in the world to have a permanent collection of famed glass artist Dale Chihuly's work. A 2004 exhibition of his work was so popular, the non-

profit organization that supports the Conservatory bought almost the entire collection for about $7 million. (*$, (614) 645-8733, fpconservatory.org*) ❹ **The Longaberger Company Home Office:** I know what you're thinking: I'm telling you to drive about an hour from campus to see a company's office building? Yes, I am. That's because Longaberger employees work in a basket. A very big basket. See, the Newark company makes baskets, and it designed its corporate headquarters to look like the Medium Market Basket it sells. Only this one is 160 times the size of the one you can buy. It is one of the most unique buildings you will ever see in your life, and, yes, you can take a tour. (*Free, (740) 322-5588, longaberger.com*)

Nighttime Fun

❶ **Brazenhead Pub:** The original Brazen Head is in Dublin, Ireland, and is the oldest bar in Europe (maybe anywhere) having served customers since the 1100s. This one is in Dublin, Ohio, but it's named for its Irish cousin. Much newer than the original, it still has a traditional pub feel with an antique reproduction interior built by Irish carpenters, imported brews, and dishes such as fish and chips and Irish lamb stew. If the weather's nice sit outside on the patio; if it isn't, sit inside by one of the three fireplaces. (*$, (614) 792-3738*) ❷ **Columbus Music Hall**: It used to be a fire house; now it's where musicians are on fire. The stage features mostly jazz and blues, but with other music tossed in now and then. In addition to hardwood and brass chandeliers inside, you'll find a Victorian-style garden outside where you can sit under the gazebo. (*$, (614) 464-0044, columbusmusichall.com*) ❸ **The Frog Bear & Wild Boar**: It's young, hip, and in the popular Arena District. If you're a sports fan, they always have a game on and are watching-party central for OSU games. The 88-foot stainless steel bar is one of Columbus's biggest, and the menu offers everything from fish to burgers and sandwiches to cheesecake. Grab a seat on the outdoor patio and you'll be in a prime spot for some of the city's best people-watching. Inside you can hear live music many nights. *AOL CityGuide* calls it the "City's Best." (*$, (614) 621-9453, frogbearbar.com*) ❹ **Our-R-Inn**: This is a college hangout the way they're supposed to be: cheap drinks, a party atmosphere, and near campus. The club has a big outdoor patio that's overflowing when the weather's good. Inside, most people stay on the first floor, but you can go upstairs if you're looking for a little more quiet. Don't come here to eat; it's basic bar munchies for the most part. Bring cash. (*$, (614) 294-9259*) ❺ **Sugar Bar**: The new sister bar to the very popular and nearby **Spice Bar**, the Sugar Bar is three distinct rooms:

a hip lounge, a dance club, and a Russian fur-themed VIP room. The décor is sleek and modern, down to the videos playing on the plasma TVs. While there is a kitchen, you don't come here for the food. You come for the four bars and the see-and-be-seen party. (*$, (614) 224-7840, sugar-bar.net*)

Shopping

❶ **Easton Town Center:** While it's a shopping center, the layout is a sort of village setting. The shops have everything you need from big-name national retailers to small boutiques, from fashion and lifestyle to home and gifts. There are also several restaurants if all the shopping makes you hungry. And if you stay late, there are a number of nightclubs and bars to occupy you. (*(614) 337-2200, eastontowncenter.com*) ❷ **The Ohio State University Bookstore:** It's a Barnes & Noble, but it's also the OSU bookstore, with more Buckeye souvenirs, gifts, and memorabilia than you'll find most anywhere else. The main store is at the corner of 11th and High Streets, but there's also a store in the Central Classroom Building on campus. In addition to fans buying swag, you'll share the aisles with students buying biology books. (*(614) 678-5664, ohiostate.bkstore.com*)

PENN STATE

Pennsylvania State University: 40,571 students
State College, PA: pop. 38,720
Beaver Stadium: seats 107,282
Colors: Blue and White
Nickname: Nittany Lions
Mascot: Nittany Lion
Phone: (800) 833-5533

RVs arrive as early as 6 p.m. Thursday, park in Yellow Lots alongside Orchard and Fox Hollow Roads. Overnight camping $50 per night, first-come, first-served. RV day-only parking $30, cars $15. Tailgating starts 8 a.m. Saturday, continues throughout game. No charcoal or wood grills; gas only. Canopies and tents prohibited in Preferred or Yellow parking areas. No kegs, beer balls, or other alcoholic beverages allowed in parking areas. No oversized inflatables, advertising banners, or displays. No weapons or fireworks; no disorderly conduct or infringing on another's area.

Shuttle Info: Free shuttles are available from downtown and South Atherton St., starting 3 hours before kickoff, until 1 hour postgame.

Nittany Lions Media Partners: 1450-AM WMAJ, 95.7-FM WMRF

What has become one of the largest public school systems in America began as a high school; Farmers' High School of Pennsylvania, specifically.

The school was founded on donated land in 1855 at the request of the Pennsylvania State Agricultural Society, but became a college a few years later when the Morrill Land-Grant Act was passed in 1862. Pennsylvania selected the school to receive the federal funds and almost immediately felt the effects of pairing agricultural studies with more classic curriculum. Students began to leave, and by 1875 only 64 were still on campus.

George Atherton is generally credited with turning that around. He became president of the university in 1882 and introduced new programs and ideas, including engineering studies. Before long Penn State was one of the nation's ten largest engineering schools.

Another university president (Ralph Hetzel) introduced another innovative idea during the Depression era. Many could no longer afford to go off to school, so he began opening satellite campuses around the state to bring classes to the students. Today there are 24 Penn State campuses, and total enrollment is more than 80,000 (half of it is on the main campus known as University Park).

Eighty thousand is a lot of people, but it's nothing compared to the crowd that pours into Happy Valley, as the area is called, for a Penn State football game. Beaver Stadium seats 107,282 and is the second largest college stadium in America. It's a long way from Beaver Field, Penn State's first football home that saw its first game in 1893. That venue had 500 seats.

The school's football program has grown along with the stadium. What began in 1887 as a collection of players competing on the grass in front of the Old Main classroom building has become one of the nation's premier football teams with four national championships (1911 and 1912 as an independent, 1982 and 1986 as a member of the Big Ten) and "Joe Pa."

"Joe Pa," of course, is Joe Paterno, who began coaching the Nittany Lions when Lyndon Johnson was in the White House. Although he became head coach in 1966, he had been an assistant coach at the school since 1950 (Harry Truman occupied the White House then, if you're keeping track). During his time at the helm, he's won more than 360 games, more than 20 bowl games, and was (along with Florida State's Bobby Bowden) inducted into the College Football Hall of Fame in 2006. The two are the first active coaches to receive the honor.

Among the players Paterno coached was John Cappelletti, who played tailback for the Nittany Lions. During his senior year in 1973, Cappelletti rushed for 1,522 yards and scored 17 touchdowns as he helped lead Penn State to an undefeated season. For his efforts he won both the Maxwell Award and the Heisman Trophy that year. His acceptance speech into the College Football Hall of Fame is still considered one of the most memorable as he dedicated his honor to his dying brother Joey. John and Joey's relationship was the subject of a book and movie, both titled *Something for Joey*.

After his collegiate career Cappelletti went on to play professionally for the Los Angeles Rams and San Diego Chargers.

Other notable Nittany Lions include Hall of Famers Jack Ham and Franco Harris.

School Mascot

There isn't really a Nittany Lion—at least as a species.

But there is a Mount Nittany, and Penn State rests in Nittany Valley. And, until they were eliminated in the late 1880s, lions did roam the mountainside. It's that combination, along with a mascot contest, that created the Nittany Lions.

It all started in 1907 when a student at the time, Joe Mason, was motivated by seeing the Princeton Tiger on a trip to the New Jersey school. Penn State didn't have a mascot, but he created the Nittany Lions in his mind and told anyone who would listen that his Penn State Nittany Lions could beat their Tigers any day.

When he returned to campus in State College, he began persuading students and the school that Penn State needed to make the Nittany Lions the official mascot. He must have been a good campaigner, because later that same year the first lion symbols started showing up on campus, and Penn State became the Nittany Lions. About the same time the first costumed mascot appeared.

"The Nittany Lion" is also one of the fight songs you'll hear the Marching Blue Band play during games. They lyrics were changed some when Penn State joined the Big Ten—the third verse referencing rivals like Michigan and Ohio State was added. The verse including old independent Penn State's rivals like Pittsburgh and Cornell is not regularly sung anymore.

"The Nittany Lion"
Every college has a legend, passed on from year to year,
To which they pledge allegiance, and always cherish dear.
But of all the honored idols, there's but one that stands the test,
It's the stately Nittany Lion, the symbol of our best.

Chorus:
HAIL! to the Lion, loyal and true.
HAIL! Alma Mater, with your white and blue.
PENN! STATE! forever, molder of men (and women),
FIGHT! for her honor—FIGHT!—and victory again.

There's Pittsburgh with its Panther,
And Penn her Red and Blue,
Dartmouth with its Indian,
And Yale her Bulldog, too.
There's Princeton with
* its Tiger,*
And Cornell with its Bear.
But speaking now of victory,
We'll get the Lion's share.

(Chorus)

Indiana has its Hoosiers,
Purdue its gold and black.
The Wildcats from
* Northwestern*
And Spartans on attack.
Ohio State has its Buckeyes,
Up north, The Wolverines.
But the mighty Nittany Lions,
The best they've ever seen.

(Chorus)

Game-Day Traditions
The Blue Band

At Penn State the Blue Band is as much a part of game day as the team is . . . only less critical to the outcome of the game. Unless you believe that drum major flip thing. But I'll get to that.

To see the spirit of the band, and of the fans for it, just take a look as tailgaters gather to listen to the band warm up and then fall in line and follow it to the Blue Bus Convoy. With the band playing—and the fans cheering—the players get off their buses and walk through the crowd into the stadium.

Inside the stadium, as the Blue Band takes the field for its pregame perform-ance, the drum major takes center stage. His two front flips have become famous, and legend has it if he sticks the flip, the Nitanny Lions will win. If not, well . . .

Visiting Penn State

State College is here for one reason: Penn State is here. The town developed to serve the needs of Pennsylvania State Farmers' High School when it opened in 1855. Today State College is driven economically and culturally by Penn State.

State College is a typical college town with the lifestyle you'd expect. That's one reason they call the area Happy Valley. And there must be something to it; in the 1980s *Psychology Today* named State College one of the least stressful places in America.

Where to Stay

❶ **Atherton Hotel:** It's a historic hotel that has been renovated to look good-as-new and offers all the modern hotel amenities. **Tarragon**, the hotel restaurant, offers dishes like Black Pepper Crusted Sea Scallops and Napoleon of Grilled Lobster Filet. Prices for rooms range from $107, if you are visiting the campus, to $128, if you aren't. (*(800) 832-0132, athertonhotel.net*) ❷ **Bellefonte/State College KOA:** It's a short drive from Penn State and won the 2004 President's award for excellence (although I'm pretty certain "Dubya" didn't have anything to do with that). The park has 140 sites, a dump station, and the usual amenities. The maximum pull-through length is 70 feet. Sites run $26–$42 depending on hookups. If you're in town for a late-season game, you'll need to go somewhere else—they close for the season in November. (*(800) 562-8127, koa.com/where/pa/38117/*) ❸ **Fort Bellefonte Campground:** This is the

closest campsite to Penn State. It's a pretty basic campground with 100 sites, full hookups, WiFi, and dumping stations. Rates range from $32–$38. (*(800) 487-9067, fortbellefonte.com*) ❹ **Great Oak Inn:** Just a couple miles from PSU, this B&B has three guestrooms with adjoining bathrooms. You can have a continental breakfast served to you in bed, or you can get out of bed and have a three-course hot breakfast in the dining room. A stay here will cost you $163–$217 during game weekends. (*(814) 867-1907, greatoakinn.com*) ❺ **Inn on the Sky:** This is the kind of place you see in *Architectural Digest* or on one of those

HGTV shows. The inn has three floors, an open floor plan, polished honey-colored wood, and exposed timbers everywhere. Each of the five guestrooms has its own bath and a great view. Rooms run $260–$310 for home-game weekends. (*(814) 422-0386, innonthesky.com*)

❻ **Nittany Lion Inn:** Stay here and you're living on campus. The Inn is listed in the National Registry of Historic Hotels, and like many older hotels the rooms are on the smallish side. But the property has been upgraded to include all the amenities you'd expect in a hotel. During home football weekends rooms run $259. (*(800) 233-7505, pshs.psu.edu/nittanylioninn/nlhome.asp*)

❼ **Reynolds Mansion:** This is more than a B&B; it's a showplace. Among the stone mansion's architectural features are an ornate staircase, carved wooden ceilings, and inlaid floors. The Mansion has 6 rooms that will cost you $185–$235 if there's a home game and will require a 2- or 3-day minimum stay. (*(800) 899-3929, reynolds mansion.com*)

ALMA MATER

For the Glory of Old State
For her founders strong and great.
For the future that we wait,
Raise the song, raise the song.

Sing our love and loyalty,
Sing our hopes that bright and free
Rest, O Mother, dear with thee
All with thee, all with thee.

When we stood at childhood's gate,
Shapeless in the hands of fate,
Thou didst mold us dear old State
Dear Old State, dear old State.

May no act of ours bring shame
To one heart that loves thy name,
May our lives but swell they fame,
Dear old State, dear old State.

Where to Eat

TAILGATER GROCERIES: ❶ **State College Farmers' Market:** This outdoor market offers produce and other supplies every Friday from June to November. You're buying directly from the source here; everything is locally grown or made. (*statecollegefarmers.org*) ❷ **Stone Soup:** Here you can stock up on fruits, vegetables, dairy products, meats, poultry, fish, eggs, and baked goods all

Buying Beer, Wine, and Spirits in Pennsylvania

Thanks to some of the most strict alcohol laws in the country, it can get confusing when trying to buy beverages for your tailgate party in Pennsylvania.

The only places to buy beer are at a beer distributor or at a six-pack store (which some call a bottle store). If you buy from a distributor, you'll find a larger selection than at the six-pack store and find some local and regional beers. But it's kind of like Costco; you buy in bulk—they don't sell anything smaller than a case. The six-pack store lets you buy beer a six-pack at a time (but the name gave that away, didn't it?). Some bars and restaurants are also allowed to sell patrons a six-pack of beer, but not all.

If you're looking for wine or "hard" liquor in Pennsylvania, look in a state store. As the name suggests, these are owned and operated by the Commonwealth of Pennsylvania, and it is the only way you can buy anything stronger than beer in this state, unless you're buying it by the glass at a bar or restaurant.

Purchasing alcohol on a Sunday is a bit of a gamble. Beer distributors and bottle stores are usually closed on Sundays, but some state stores are open. Best to stock up early.

locally produced. Participating farms practice sustainable agriculture, and most of the produce is organic. Also on the shelves are homemade body-care products, specialty foods, and works by local artisans. (*(814) 234-3135, stonesoupmarket.org*)

SPORTS BARS: ❸ **Champ's Sports Bar and Grill:** Bring your tailgate neighborhood here; a renovation doubled the size of this popular place. One of the things that makes it popular is the fact there are 70 TVs. On the menu you'll find dishes you'd expect at a sports bar. (*$, (814) 237-6010, champssportsgrill.com*) ❹ **The Sports Center Café & Grille:** If you picture a typical, college-town sports bar, chances are it will look something like The Sports Center. Six TVs, cheap beer, and inexpensive food makes this a popular student hangout on game days. (*$, (814) 234-2299*)

RESTAURANTS: **❺ Duffy's Boalsburg Tavern:** It may sound like one place, but it's really two: the more upscale **Boalsburg Tavern** and the pub-style **Duffy's Tavern**. Duffy's operated continuously from 1819 until 1934 when a fire damaged the building. It was restored, and its present appearance and condition are recorded in the Library of Congress. If you visit, take a look at the walls. They're 22-inch-thick stone walls that keep summer's indoor temperatures around 69 degrees; no need for AC. (*$, (814) 466-6241, duffystavern.com*)

❻ Gamble Mill Restaurant: This converted mill is more than 220 years old. Inside you'll find exposed brick, fieldstone, and mortar walls with wood panels and some plaster. The building's massive timbers are exposed and set off, as are door frames, with bundles of birch saplings seeded with lights. You'll also find a menu that takes you from France to Asia, with several stops in between. They also offer an award-winning wine list. (*$$, (814) 355-7764, gamblemill.com*)

❼ The Goppers: It has a bit of a hippie feel and serves up pizza, stromboli, pasta, sandwiches, and subs. But the basics work here, as the place is very popular with students and locals. They offer takeout and delivery if you want someone else to do your tailgate cooking. (*$, (814) 234-1606, goppers.com*)

❽ Penn State Creamery: This is where Ben and Jerry learned to make ice cream. Sort of. Penn State is well respected for its dairy farming research, and the Creamery is a side benefit. There are more than 110 flavors of super-premium ice

cream here. And while Ben and Jerry didn't actually learn to make ice cream on the premises, they did take a correspondence course through Penn State to learn about ice cream production. (*$, (814) 865-7535, creamery.psu.edu/creamery.html*)

❾ **Ye Old College Diner:** On campus they just call it the Diner. It's where students and locals have been going for breakfast for more than 70 years. They're famous for grilled stickies—a square, gooey sticky bun that's been split, brushed with butter, and then grilled. They also serve meals other than breakfast. (*$, (814) 238-5590, thediner.statecollege.com*)

Daytime Fun

❶ **Brookmere Winery:** You don't think of Pennsylvania as the wine country, but there are a number of wineries in the area. Many have tours, but Brookmere's is considered one of the best, and it's not far from campus. Part of the tour includes a tasting, and you can pick up a bottle or other gift in their shop. If you bring a large group, call ahead and they'll prepare a private tour for you. (*Free, (717) 935-5380, brookmerewine.com*) ❷ **Cavern Tours:** Thanks to geology, this part of the world has lots of caverns. Thanks to entrepreneurs, you can tour many of them. You can learn about all the caverns at goodearthgraphics.com/showcave/pa.html, but here are three of the more popular tours. **Indian Caverns:** These caverns are a huge series of rooms, tunnels, and passageways with stunning formations and the only ones in the world that glow in the dark. That's from the radium deposits that twinkle like stars. (*$, (814) 632-7578, indiancaverns.com*) **Lincoln Caverns:** Lincoln Caverns is a smaller cave system, but you can strike it rich here. Visitors can pan for real gemstones from mid-March through mid-November . . . but don't expect to find enough to quit your job. (*$–$$, (814) 643-0268, lincolncaverns.com*) **Penn's Cave:** You take this tour by boat since the cave system lies half-submerged by underground springs. The motorboat tour takes about an hour. The water is full of trout, and you can also take a wildlife tour on a safari bus to see native Northeastern animals such as deer, elk, and wild turkeys. (*$, (814) 364-1664, pennscave.com*) ❸ **Columbus Chapel and Boal Mansion Museum:** You can thank the Boals for Penn State. That's because the Boal family moved here after the Revolutionary War and founded the school that became Penn State. The mansion tour showcases rooms reflecting fashions from the late 1700s to the Gilded Age of the early 1900s. Be sure to see the chapel of Christopher Columbus. This is the *actual* chapel moved piece by piece from Europe. (*$, (814) 466-6210, boalmuseum.com*)

❹ **Palmer Museum of Art:** Located on campus, the museum has 11 galleries, a print-study room, 150-seat auditorium, and outdoor sculpture garden. Included in the permanent collection are works by a number of A-list European and American artists. They also feature rotating exhibits throughout the year. (*Free, (814) 865-*

7672, psu.edu/dept/
palmermuseum)

**❺ The Sky's the Limit
Balloon Company:** This is
just plain fun. These hot-air
balloon rides last about an
hour, and once back on the
ground, you enjoy a cham-
pagne toast to congrat-
ulate yourself. If it's your
first time up, you'll get a
flight certificate to prove
you did it. It's not cheap
($175 per person), but it's
a great view from up
there. (*$$$, (814) 234-5986,
paballoonrides.com*)

Nighttime Fun

❶ The Crowbar: This is a
student favorite for live
rock music. Most of the acts are regional or on the college circuit, but some of
them (such as Matchbox 20 and Train) went on to become stars. In addition to
music you'll find pool tables and plenty of drink specials. (*$–$$, (814) 237-0426,
crowbarlivemusic.com*) **❷ The Gingerbread Man:** This place gets packed at
night with PSU students enjoying cheap food and drinks. The G-Man has a small
dance floor and is a popular Greek hangout. During the day it's a pretty popular
restaurant, too. (*$, (814) 237-0361, gmanstatecollege.com*) **❸ The Hotel State
College:** No, it's not a real college, and there are no tests—unless you count
remembering what goes in a Vampire's Kiss. **Allen St. Grill, The Corner Room,
Players Nite Club,** and **Zeno's Pub** are all located within the Hotel State
College. The Corner Room on the first floor serves casual food; upstairs, Allen
Street Grill has a more upscale menu. Players and Zeno's are popular places for

a drink and dance. (And if you need help with that Vampire's Kiss test, the answer is vodka, gin, dry vermouth, tequila, salt, and tomato juice.) (*$, (814) 231-GRIL, allenstreetgrill.com*) ❹ **Otto's Pub and Brewery:** A bit away from the campus scene, this microbrewery offers seasonally changing beer selections. It also offers a full menu with both the basics and nontraditional dishes such as Pretzel-crusted Catfish and Helles-battered Tofu Filet. (*$, (814) 867-6886, ottospubandbrewery.com*) ❺ **The Rathskellar:** It opened in 1933 and ever since has been the favorite bar of Penn State alums. It's just a hole-in-the-wall joint filled with memorabilia, but cheap beer and eats keep them coming in. Don't let it confuse you, but the dinner menu is an abbreviated version of the lunch menu. Go figure. (*$, (814) 237-3858, theskeller.com*)

Shopping

❶ **The Gallery Shop:** Artists working in wood, metal, jewelry, textiles, paper, and more sell their works here—more than 50 artists, in fact. Many of the pieces focus on Pennsylvania heritage. (*(814) 867-0442, gallery-shop.com*)
❷ **Old State Clothing Co.:** If it has a Nittany Lion or the letters *P-S-U* on it, you'll find it here. In addition to the usual apparel and souvenirs, Old State has several unique gifts with a Penn State twist. (*(888) 234-1415, oldstate.com*)

❸ **Plaza Centre Antique Gallery and Ritz Gift Mall:** It used to be a theater; now it's a co-op mall with antiques, collectibles, vintage clothing, and arts and crafts. There are also some standard retail shops here. If you need more inventory to browse, go next door to the **Ritz Theatre,** which has more shops. (*(814) 357-4870, geocities.com/plazacentre/*)

PURDUE

Purdue University: 37,871 students
West Lafayette, IN: pop. 28,778
Ross Ade Stadium: seats 62,500
Colors: Old Gold and Black
Nickname: Boilermakers
Mascot: Boilermaker Special, Purdue Pete, and Rowdy
Phone: (800) 497-7878

Non-permit RVs can park 6 p.m. Friday night in IM Black Lot, $30. Tailgating starts about 4 hours before game, and continues throughout. No tailgating or shuttle service in free lots. Visit Boilermaker Streetfest alongside Mackey Arena for pregame family friendly activities, like inflatable games. You can meet the team, too.

Shuttle Info: Shuttles available only for John Purdue Club members parked in the new U Lot. Shuttle is free.

Boilermakers Media Partners: 95.3-FM WLFF, 1410-AM WLAS

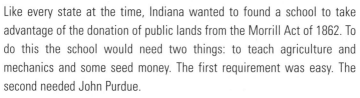

Like every state at the time, Indiana wanted to found a school to take advantage of the donation of public lands from the Morrill Act of 1862. To do this the school would need two things: to teach agriculture and mechanics and some seed money. The first requirement was easy. The second needed John Purdue.

John Purdue was a successful businessman in Lafayette, as well as a noted philanthropist. In 1865 he agreed to donate $150,000—to go with $50,000 from Tippecanoe County—to found the university that would take his name. If Purdue were to make that contribution in today's dollars, it would be more than $1.5 million.

Nine years later, in 1874, with 3 buildings, 6 instructors, and 39 students, Purdue was open for business.

Over the years the school widened its curriculum beyond agriculture and mechanics. Where it made its mark was in aviation. Purdue was the first university in the country to offer majors in aviation and it—as well as students and staff—has played a major role in America's aviation history.

One of those staff members was Amelia Earhart. The famed aviator is best known, of course, for her attempt to fly around the world. Her plane, and the project, were financed by Purdue where she joined the staff in 1935 as Counselor of Careers for Women. She left Purdue University Airport in her Lockheed L-10 Electra aircraft for the "Flying Laboratory" world flight that began in Miami on June 1, 1937. Her plane disappeared July 2 on a leg of the journey between New Guinea and Howland Island in the Pacific. Purdue's libraries maintain an extensive collection about Earhart and her fateful flight.

In addition to its aviation program, Purdue is nationally recognized for its engineering, agriculture, and management programs and is the largest university in Indiana.

Purdue's football team is often more recognized for its alumni than for team accomplishments. Since the school's first game in 1887 (the only game that season and a loss) the Boilermakers have often played solid football but have racked up only seven conference championships. Purdue did put together a string of successive bowl game appearances from 1997 to 2004.

Some of those famous football alumni are why Purdue has been called the "Cradle of Quarterbacks." Hall of Famers Bob Griese and Len Dawson, along with Drew Brees, Jim Everett, Mark Herrmann, and Kyle Orton, all led the Boilermakers' offense. Another famous Purdue alum also has a place in the Pro Football Hall of Fame, legendary Kansas City Chiefs coach Hank Stram.

School Mascot

No, Purdue's nickname doesn't come from the drink. It comes from a reporter for the *Crawfordsville Daily Argus News* who wrote in 1891 about Purdue's resounding 44–0 victory over Wabash College. The headline read: "Slaughter of Innocents: Wabash Snowed Completely Under by the Burly Boiler Makers from Purdue."

It wasn't long before Lafayette newspapers started using the phrase, and the following year the school newspaper adopted the name. Since then Purdue's been the Boilermakers. And if you're wondering what nicknames Boilermakers replaced, they included Haymakers, Rail-Splitters, and Cornfield Sailors.

The first Boilermakers mascot rode the rails in 1940—literally. The school wanted to adopt a mascot that glorified Purdue's engineering and railroading heritage. The first suggestion as a mascot was called "mechanical man." It was scrapped in favor of a locomotive on an automobile chassis called the Boilermaker Special. The locomotive you'll see on game day is the Boilermaker Special V.

Not far away will be another Purdue mascot: Purdue Pete. He began not as a cheerleader for the team but as a sales tool for the University Bookstore.

At the same time they were building the Boilermaker Special, the bookstore hired local artist Art Evans to draw a character to use as an advertising icon for the bookstore. Four years later, in 1944, the university yearbook used Purdue Pete on its cover. The costumed mascot started roaming the sidelines in 1956 in a head made of papiermâché draped over chicken wire. Today Purdue Pete's head is fiberglass. He also has a friend: Rowdy. The 10-foot-tall inflatable mascot was introduced in 1997.

Game-Day Traditions
Big Bass Drum

This is one big drum. They say it's the biggest drum in the world. More on that in a bit.

The drum made its debut in 1921 and stands 10 feet tall on its field carriage. It's 8 feet in diameter and 4 feet wide between the drum heads. The drum you'll see on the field is the same one that rolled out of the factory in 1921, but there is one difference. The original drum heads were made of South American mammoth steer hides; today they're synthetic. Over the years celebrities, presidents, musicians, and other famed folks have signed the drum heads, and the old ones are kept safe in the Band Department.

Now, about the title of "the world's largest drum." In 1961 the University of Texas—which says its Big Bertha bass drum is the largest in the world—

challenged Purdue's claim to the title. The showdown was to be at the Kappa Kappa Psi/Tau Beta Sigma national convention in Wichita, Kansas. Purdue's Big Bass Drum showed up, Big Bertha didn't, and Purdue's drum was crowned the "World's Largest."

Incidentally, he has nothing to do with the Big Bass Drum (he played tuba), but Orville Redenbacher played in the Purdue band. That bit of trivia should win you a drink sometime, maybe a Boilermaker.

Purdue Fight Song

Hail, hail to old Purdue!
All hail to our old gold and black!
Hail, hail to old Purdue!
Our friendship may she never lack,
Ever grateful ever true,
Thus we raise our song anew,
Of the days we've spent with you,
All hail our own Purdue.

Visiting Purdue

The small village of Chauncey knew it was going to have problems providing infrastructure for the new Purdue University, which would open in 1874. So in 1871 it voted to be annexed by Lafayette. Lafayette said no. But it turned out that the growth of the university spurred the growth of the town, which merged

with two other villages in 1888 to form West Lafayette. Today this college town is still fueled by Purdue University as well as the Purdue Research Park, which includes more than 140 companies.

Where to Stay

❶ **Commandant's Home Bed & Breakfast:** Built in 1895, this Classical Revival building is the restored and authentically furnished former residence of the Indiana Veterans' Home's leaders. This B&B has six guestrooms with private baths, each named after a noted Commandant. Rooms are pleasantly furnished, with a sensible mix of antique and modern furnishings. Rooms run $95–$145, depending on the room and whether you're staying on a weekday or weekend. (*(877) 319-2783, commhomeb-b.com*) ❷ **Loeb House Inn:** Guests find this red-brick Italianate home looks pretty much the same as when it was built in 1882. Its original owner had crazy things like an indoor toilet, central heat, and a burglar alarm installed—the neighbors thought he was nuts. Today the house has five tastefully decorated guestrooms with fireplaces, comfortable sitting areas, whirlpool or claw foot tubs, king- or queen-sized beds, and TVs. You'll get breakfast and a Victorian-style afternoon tea with homemade sweets from a local deli. Rooms run $95–$175. (*(765) 420-7737, loebhouseinn.com*) ❸ **Perrin House Bed & Breakfast:** This Civil War–era, three-story house offers four large guestrooms with private baths. Outside, the building is a combination of Italianate and Victorian styles—odd, but attractive. The guestrooms have some creative touches, like a buffalo hide comforter and Hopi drum in one room and a claw-foot tub equipped with a champagne bubble Jacuzzi in another. Guests get breakfast in the morning and tea service in the afternoon. Rooms run $95–$145. Football weekends go fast; they suggest reserving your room 6 months in advance. (*(765) 420-7628, perrinhouse.net*) ❹ **Prophetstown State Recreation Area:** In nearby Battle

Ground, this state park offers 110 sites, 55 with full hookups. Sites are surrounded by blue spruce and other trees, offering a good deal of privacy. Since it's a state park, you won't find telephone, cable, or Internet hookups here. But you will find deer right outside your door, a paved 3-mile bike path, cedar bath house, nearby historic battlefield, historic farm, and Native American village. Sites cost $17–$38, depending on full or partial utilities, and weekday or weekend stays. (*(765) 567-4919, in.gov/dnr/parklake/properties/park_prophetstown.html*) ❺ **Union Club Hotel:** Located on campus in Purdue's Memorial Union, adjacent to the Stewart Center conference facility, the Union Club has 192 rooms, including 58 deluxe accommodations. The hotel offers high-speed Internet access, free garage parking, airport shuttle service, an exercise facility, and breakfast room service. Since the hotel is attached to the student union, guests can also avail themselves of the on-site restaurants, bowling alley, billiards, and amusement games at the recreation center. Rooms run $122–$142 during football weekends. (*(800) 320-6291, hotel.purdue.edu/*)

Where to Eat

TAILGATE SUPPLIES: ❶ **Lafayette Farmers' Market:** This outdoor market space on 5th Street, between Main and Columbia, has been used to sell fresh produce, flowers, and baked goods since the 1830s. More than 35 vendors offer a wide variety of fresh, seasonal produce, baked goods, preserves, herbs, meats and eggs, and handmade items. The market is open until the end of October. (*(765) 742-2313, lafayettefarmersmarket.com*)

SPORTS BARS: ❷ **Harry's Chocolate Shop:** One of Purdue's most popular bars, it's been around since 1919 when it was a soda shop. It's a favorite bar for alums, who literally line up around the block on game days to get inside. What you'll find inside is a scruffy dive bar, with layers of graffiti covering the brick walls, a pressed tin ceiling, and sports pictures autographed by players and coaches. The menu is classic bar fare. If anyone approaches you holding a can of whipped cream, run away. You think I'm kidding . . . (*$, (765) 743-1467, harryschocolateshop.com*) ❸ **Luxie's Pub-n-Grub:** It's a gathering place, a sports bar, and a university hangout. This bi-level bar and grill has a cluster of TVs by the bar area, exposed brick walls, and room to maneuver, though it can still get pretty crowded. The east wall is covered with enormous vintage signs—advertisements for long-gone businesses painted directly onto the brick. When Luxie's was remodeled in the mid-90s, workers removed old drywall, uncovering what had once been an exterior wall. The wall served as a billboard more than 140 years ago, and is almost perfectly preserved. If you're hungry, the kitchen prepares a selection of sandwiches, burgers, and entrées. (*$, (765) 742-4782, luxies.com*) ❹ **Riehle Bros. Athletic Club:** You'll notice loads of TV screens throughout Riehle's, but the one you'll remember is their 200-inch monster. Rest assured you'll be able to see the game. This popular bar also has sand-court volleyball, shuffleboard, and a dance floor, plus weekly live bands and karaoke parties every Thursday. The cooks turn out prime rib, grilled salmon, and filet in addition to a lengthy sandwich menu. Don't just come for lunch or dinner; Riehle's also has one of the best breakfasts in town. (*$, (765) 474-4499, riehlebros.com*)

RESTAURANTS: ❺ **Azteca Restaurant:** This upscale restaurant serves a blend of Mexican and European-inspired dishes—everything from homemade chiles rellenos and hand-rolled chicken flautas to herb-crusted rack of lamb and Caldo

Siete Mares (a spicy seafood broth). The dining room sports a funky, Latin aesthetic. Azteca offers impressive wine and beer lists, along with mescals and cognacs. Reservations are suggested. (*$–$$, (765) 429-8488*) ❻ **Heisei Restaurant:** The menu is traditional Japanese fine dining, with entrées like broiled eel, shabu-shabu (sliced ribeye beef and vegetables cooked tableside), and ginger-and-soy-sautéed pork. Of course, there's sushi, generously portioned and beautifully presented. The restaurant's interior is as traditional as its menu, with rice paper screens, artful prints, and tatami rooms. (*$, (765) 463-1682, heiseirestaurant.com*) ❼ **Mountain Jack's Steakhouse:** The décor is kind of '70s rustic, casual in a ski-lodge kind of way, but still fancy enough for a night on the town. Menu highlights include Australian lobster tails, black-bleu ribeye steak, and BBQ baby back ribs. Servers bring the salad bar to you, assembling your greens at the table. (*$–$$, (765) 448-1521, paragonsteak.com*)

Daytime Fun

❶ **Art Museum of Greater Lafayette:** In 1909 a group of 25 residents created the Lafayette Art Association (the predecessor of the museum), and within a month there were 386 members who paid $1 in annual dues to belong to the organization. Nearly 100 years later the museum's collection centers on 19th-

and 20th-century American art with particular focus on art from and about Indiana. (*Free, (765) 742-1128, glmart.org*) ❷ **Imagination Station:** With interactive exhibits featuring everything from dinosaurs to computers, this children's museum provides kids, and their parents, hands-on activities to explore science, space, and technology. You can also take the controls in one of three flight simulators. (*$, (765) 420-7780, users.nlci.com/imagination*) ❸ **Red Crown Mini Museum:** They call this a "walk-by" museum, and that's exactly what you do, but it's also a step back in time. This Standard Oil Service Station was built in 1928 and used glazed brick for the walls and tile for the roof; it was an expensive gas station for the time, and there are just seven of them left anywhere. In the windows are displays of automobile and service station memorabilia. If you're wondering about the name, the station pumped mostly Red Crown gasoline. (*No contact information, but it is at the corner of South and 6th Streets in Lafayette*) ❹ **Tippecanoe Battlefield:** Just north of Lafayette is the Tippecanoe Battlefield, which was where in 1811 Native Americans lost control of their Midwestern lands and William Henry Harrison, who led the battle against the Indians, began his path

to the White House ("Tippecanoe and Tyler, too"). Visitors can walk the battlefield where settlers and Native Americans clashed, as well as learn more in the museum. (*$, (765) 476-8411, tcha.mus. in.us/battlefield.htm*)

Nighttime Fun

❶ **Cox's Pub:** Okay, let's see what you've got. Cox's is all karaoke, all the time. That's right, you can sing seven nights a week to more than 4,000 songs in

what's been named the #1 Karaoke Bar in Lafayette (no surprise, huh?). The menu can feed you from breakfast to dinner, and if you don't sing you can play pool, darts, and video games. They also put ball games on the big screen. (*$, (765) 742-8727, coxspub.com*) ❷ **Lafayette Brewing Company:** Located in a restored, historic building in Lafayette, LBC is a favorite hangout for those wanting to kick back, have a beer, maybe eat something, and enjoy their evening. The beers are the stars here, of course, including local legends like the Eastside Bitter and the Black Angus Oatmeal Stout. Upstairs is a pizza kitchen and where you'll find live entertainment ranging from music to comics. (*$, (765) 742-2591, lafayettebrewingco.com*) ❸ **Neon Cactus:** They have the largest dance floor in the area, and on Thursday nights a 32-ounce glass of beer costs you a dime. Yep, 10 cents. I bet that helps get people dancing. Besides the beer the Neon Cactus has a martini lounge (they call it Ne), and in the Piano Room the interactive show requires audience participation. The menu has rotating drink specials along with bar food and sandwiches. (*$, (765) 743-6081, neoncactus.biz*) ❹ **Where Else Bar:** Located downtown, this is the kind of college bar that comes to mind when you hear those words. Lots of drink specials, DJs and a dance floor, and Big Ten football watching keeps the place crowded. (*$, (765) 746-1122*)

Shopping

❶ **Downtown Lafayette/West Lafayette:** More than 70 shops line the streets of historic downtown. Antique, gift, and hobby shops share the spotlight with art, household, and apparel stores. (*(800) 872-6648, lafayettewestlafayette downtown.com*)   ❷ **Purdue University Bookstore:** Just on the edge of campus, this is where you can find all your Boilermaker gear. And not just clothing and tailgate gear. You can get a nice recliner and ottoman set with the train logo, pick up a Joe Tiller bobblehead, or take to the links a sleeve of white, gold, and black logoed golf balls. You can also get textbooks here if you feel like learning something. (*(800) 347-9618, purdueu.com*)

WISCONSIN

University of Wisconsin: 41,219 students
Madison, WI: pop. 221,551
Camp Randall Stadium: seats 76,634
Colors: Cardinal and White
Nickname: Badgers
Mascot: Bucky
Phone: (800) GO-BADGERS

RVs and all oversized vehicles park in Lot 51 only, at the corner of Mills and Regent Streets, $40. Purchase parking permits in advance through UW Athletic Ticket Office (608) 262-1440. No overnight parking. Lot 34 is an alcohol-free tailgating zone. Shuttles are provided, $4 round trip. Tailgating starts first thing game day, continues throughout game.

Shuttle Info: Two Bucky Bus shuttle routes run on game day to and from Camp Randall Stadium. Shuttles run every 15 to 18 minutes, starting 2 hours prior to kickoff until 1 hour postgame, $4 per person round trip. Shuttle picks up at bus stop between Lot 60 and Lot 76, and any of the six Capitol Square parking ramps.

Badgers Media Partners: 101.1-FM and 1310-AM WIBA

When Wisconsin was admitted into the Union, its founding constitution called for a state university "at or near the seat of state government." That was in 1848, and the next year the University of Wisconsin opened—although classes were held at the Madison Female Academy. The first university buildings wouldn't be built until 1851.

The next several decades were ones of growth for the university, including expansion of programs and curriculum. But the decade of the 1960s was marked by student protests and violence mostly in protest of the Vietnam War.

The worst of the protests were from 1966 to 1970 with the first major demonstration protesting the presence of Dow Chemical recruiters on campus. Dow supplied the military with napalm used in the war. Authorities used force to break up the protest, injuring several students. The scene later found its way to television in the PBS documentary *Two Days in October* and was the topic of the book *They Marched into Sunlight*.

The period of protest on campus came to a violent and deadly end in 1970. The target was the Army Math Research Center on campus. At 3:40 a.m. on August 24, four men who were or had been associated with the university pulled a van filled with an ammonium nitrate and fuel mixture next to Sterling Hall, which housed the Research Center. The explosion damaged much of the building and killed a graduate student researcher who was working late to finish some work before leaving on vacation.

The school recovered from this period, of course, and its academic standing among public universities has continued to improve.

Its reputation as a party school has, too. Wisconsin ranks as the country's number one party school according to the *Princeton Review* and *Playboy* magazine. The campus is also where juniors Tim Keck and Christopher Johnson founded the parody newspaper *The Onion*.

The Wisconsin football program was founded in 1889, although the inaugural campaign wasn't one to brag about. The Badgers went 0-2. But things got better.

Wisconsin was a founding member of the Big Ten in 1896 and won the first two conference championships. They've won the title ten more times in the years since. The Badgers have also produced two of the best college football players in history.

Lino Dante Amici was born in Italy but moved to Kenosha, Wisconsin, in the 1930s where his cousins Don and Jim Ameche lived. That is why football fans know this Heisman Trophy winner by the name Alan Ameche.

Ameche was also known as "The Horse," and in his years at Wisconsin, he played both sides of the ball as fullback and linebacker. It was the fullback part that won him accolades as he gained 3,212 yards during his career, setting an NCAA record. In 1953 he came in sixth in the Heisman voting; in 1954 he came in first.

Wisconsin's other Heisman winner also set an NCAA rushing record: 6,397 yards, breaking the old record during his last game as a Badger. That back was Ron Dayne, though fans and broadcasters called him "The Great Dayne." And when you add in bowl game performances—he had some great ones—his rushing total was 7,125 yards, making him the first back in collegiate football to rush for more than 7,000 yards.

School Mascot

His name is Buckingham U. Badger, but you can call him Bucky. Everyone else does.

The Badger nickname is borrowed from Wisconsin—the Badger State—although there is some debate about whether that came from the animal or a reference to the way some early settlers lived. There's no debate that the animal represents the university.

An actual, live badger was first used as a mascot, but it was too difficult to control and could get mean at times, so it was sent packing to a nearby zoo. His replacement: a live raccoon named Regdab (that's Badger spelled backward). Don't ask. It didn't last long.

The first illustrated badger was drawn by a local Wisconsin artist in 1940 and went by various names including Benny, Buddy, and Bouncey. He came to life as a costumed mascot in 1949. At the same time a naming contest came up with the formal Buckingham U. Badger.

Bucky was popular around Madison and even used by many businesses as a part of their logo and advertising. In fact, the university had to go to court in 1988 to fight for a trademark on the Bucky logo. The court agreed with the university. They were happy; those businesses weren't.

It should be noted that in 1973 Wisconsin's assistant attorney general tried to kill off Bucky. Well, at least fire him. Howard Koop was his name, and he proposed that Bucky be replaced by with Henrietta Holstein, a cow. His argument, "kids love cows." After all, this is America's Dairyland and the state where a legislator once proposed to change the saying on the state license plate to "Eat Cheese or Die."

Both Henrietta Holstein and the license plate proposals failed.

Game-Day Traditions
The Fifth Quarter

Most stadiums clear out after the final whistle. Not Camp Randall. As many as 30,000 fans hang around for the Fifth Quarter. It all began in the late 1970s when the Badger Band created its unique postgame show. In addition to a review of the band's performances from its pregame show, they began performing arrangements that included the fans (be prepared to sing and dance along with "Beer Barrel Polka," the "Chicken Dance," and "Space Badgers," among others), playing while lying on the ground, or standing on their heads—basically doing whatever they wanted. The fans loved it, the media started calling it the Fifth Quarter, and now it's a Badger tradition.

Visiting Wisconsin

Madison is the state capital and often high on all those lists of the best places to live. The university and state government dominate the economy, although

Oscar Mayer is based here, as are a growing number of high-tech companies. The outdoors is popular here, especially cycling; there is an extensive bike trail system throughout the city. That may be one reason *Men's Journal* named Madison the healthiest city in America in 2004. There's also an active nightlife in town . . . probably one reason *Playboy* named Wisconsin the nation's top party school in 2006.

Where to Stay

❶ **Arbor Inn:** With eight comfortable guestrooms, this environmental inn makes going "green" look good. The inn consists of a 100-year-old stone farmhouse, and a modern annex built using recycled and eco-friendly materials. Rooms have private baths stocked with Aveda products and are furnished in a mix of country and neo-Shaker styles. Some rooms have organic mattresses and bed linens. The inn is across the street from the UW arboretum. Rooms run $125–$230 during football and other event weekends. (*(608) 238-2981, arbor-house.com*)

❷ **The Dahlmann Campus Inn:** This boutique-style hotel, with its impressive marble lobby, is located on campus. The warm-toned rooms are filled with mahogany furniture and European accents along with other amenities like free high-speed Internet access and a morning paper. Guests start out the day with a complimentary continental breakfast. During Big Ten game weekends rooms run $192–$410; non-conference game weekends are $10 cheaper. (*(800) 589-6285, thecampusinn.com*) ❸ **Lake Farm Park:** This 54-site RV park is part of Capital

Springs Centennial State Park & Recreation Area. Thirty-nine of Lake Farm's sites have electric hookups, bathroom and shower facilities, and a dump station. Sites here run $22. (*(608) 242-4576, countyofdane.com/lwrd/parks/parklist.asp*)

❹ **Madison Concourse Hotel:** This 13-story hotel just north of Capitol Square is filled with large windows and an elegant lobby. Guestrooms are decorated in an upscale colonial style, with wireless Internet access and Nintendo for gamers. One hundred rooms are part of the "Governor's Club" on the top three floors, offering the best views, as well as appetizers, cocktails, and other little extras. During football weekends, rooms on all levels run from $184 to $239. (*(800) 356-8293, concoursehotel.com*) ❺ **Mansion Hill Inn:** Four blocks from the Capitol, this 1857 German Romanesque Revival mansion has a 4-story spiral staircase and 11 individually decorated rooms so nice you might not want to leave to see the game. Okay, not *that* nice. But the rooms do range from large to huge; among them the Atomic Room (with minimalist, 50s'-style furniture, a plasma TV, and steam shower) and the Oriental Suite (with separate sitting room, King-size bed, a skylight, and double whirlpool). Rates for football weekends run $205–$325 with a two-night minimum stay. (*(800) 798-9070, mansionhillinn.com*)

Where to Eat

TAILGATE SUPPLIES: ❶ **The Dane County Farmers' Market:** Vendors line the Capitol Square selling fresh produce, meats, eggs and dairy, baked goods, preserves, and other treats. The outdoor market is open Wednesdays and Saturdays from July to November. The rest of the year, it moves indoors at the Monona Terrace. (*(608) 455-1999, madfarmmkt.org*) ❷ **Woodman's Food Market:** This regional, employee-owned supermarket carries 70,000 items, compared to the 15,000 stocked by typical supermarkets. That bulk purchasing helps keep prices at Woodman's about 10 to 20 percent cheaper than many competitors. (*(608) 244-6630*)

SPORTS BARS: ❸ **Lucky's Bar & Grill:** Just a few blocks from Camp Randall, Lucky's is a popular destination for sports lovers. With 40 TVs hanging everywhere possible (and sports memorabilia hanging where TVs aren't), plus interactive TV game shows, dart boards, and a Lucky's 16 Shuffleboard, the bar stays busy game or no game. Daily lunch specials, burgers, and homemade pizzas will curb your hunger. (*$, (608) 250-8989, luckysmadison.com*) ❹ **Pooley's:** This neighborhood bar touts itself as Madison's largest and most interactive sports bar. As proof,

Pooley's offers up its massive 8 x 10-foot big screen, viewable from a specially assigned Sky Box. There's also an extended satellite system allowing viewers to watch multiple games on one screen. The walls are plastered with sports memorabilia of all kinds, including photos, helmets, news clippings, and some unused tickets from famous games. The kitchen's open late and includes bar-fare classics. There's also a kid's menu. (*$, (608) 242-1888, foodspot.com/pooleys*)

❺ **State Street Brats:** Named one of the country's 25 best sports bars in 2005 by *Sports Illustrated*, this bar's recipe for success is founded on cold beer, hot bratwursts, and a multitude of TVs. In fact, one of their monitors is so big it's surrounded by tiered seats so everybody gets a good view. On game days students, alums, and locals cheer on their Badgers, while washing down brats and cheese curds (don't ask) with pints of Spotted Cow or Leinenkugel's amid the Badgerabilia. (*$, (608) 255-5544, statestreetbrats.com*)

RESTAURANTS: ❻ **The Blue Marlin:** In the main dining room, striking stained glass windows echo the shape of a leaping marlin. Outside, additional tables are arranged for diners on the square. The menu changes depending on what's available, but you'll usually find blue marlin (of course), tuna, salmon, Alaskan halibut, swordfish, or Chilean sea bass listed. The kitchen showcases the fish's flavors by simple grilling, then accenting with light sauces or a brush of aromatics. There's also shellfish and a raw bar. (*$$, (608) 255-2255, thebluemarlin.net*)

❼ Delaney's Charcoal Steaks: Serving some of the finest steaks in Madison, this steakhouse is long on quality and short on pretension. A stone's throw from West Towne Mall, the restaurant provides a variety of Black Angus steaks, chops, and prime rib. You'll also find chicken, lobster, pork, lamb, fish, and pasta dishes on the menu. Unlike many steak houses, Delaney's entrées include some side items. Locals recommend the homemade onion rings, too. (*$$, (608) 833-7337, foodspot.com/delaneys/index.html*) **❽ Essen Haus:** Catering to Madison's large German population, this Teutonic restaurant and beer hall serves traditional dishes, like wiener schnitzel, sauerbraten, orange-glazed duck, and a variety of wursts. The staff wears authentic costumes, and oompah music floats (okay, bounces) through the air. Beer lovers can choose from 16 German varieties on tap or more than 200 international brands. (*$–$$, (608) 255-4674, essen-haus.com*) **❾ Weary Traveler Free House:** While the menu is diverse enough to please the most militant vegan, easily the most popular item is Bob's Bad Breath Burger, a patty adorned with caramelized onions, garlic, and cream cheese on a tender roll. Also on hand are two-fisted sandwiches stuffed with tuna or lamb, hearty goulash, ceviche, and pork chops. The casual publike atmosphere includes random pictures, signs, and props nailed to the walls that provide conversation starters. (*$, (608) 442-6207*)

Daytime Fun

❶ Betty Lou Cruises: For cocktails, brunch, or dinner, you can cruise either Lake

Mendota or Lake Monoma for a couple of hours and enjoy Madison from the water. Dinner cruises are on Sunday only, but call ahead because they often have special cruises (last fall Thursday nights offered pizza and beer cruises). Betty Lou was the mother of the guys who run the company now, which is part of the family business that also owns several other waterfront businesses and restaurants. (*$$$, (608) 246-3138, bettyloucruises.com*) ❷ **Chazen Museum of Art:** Paintings from 1300 up to today sit alongside sculptures, photography, and contemporary art at the UW-Madison's Chazen Museum of Art. Complementing the permanent collection are traveling exhibitions highlighting specific artists, periods, and media. (*Free, (608) 263-2246, chazen.wisc.edu*) ❸ **Henry Vilas Zoo:** This is one of just a handful of zoo's in the country that doesn't charge admission. That was one of the requirements Col. William and Anna Vilas had in 1904 when they donated the land and much of the money to build the zoo, named for their son who died at a young age. In addition to the lions, giraffes, penguins, and the like, there's a Children's Zoo

where little humans can feed little animals. (*Free, (608) 266-4733, vilaszoo.org*)

❹ **Hinchley's Dairy Farm Tour:** This is the Dairy State so why not see why? The Hinchley's have been giving tours of their farm since 1998, and visitors get to take it all in from an antique-tractor-driven hayride through the fields. You can also pet and feed goats and sheep, gather eggs in the henhouse, and even milk a cow. Tours end for the season after Halloween. (*$–$$, (608) 764-5090, dairyfarmtours.com*)

❺ **Huber Brewery:** About an hour's drive from Madison,

you'll find the oldest continuously operating brewery in the Midwest, and the second oldest in the country. Huber filled its first keg in 1845. The brewery's Berghoff Beer is its best-known brand, first brewed for the Chicago restaurant of the same name in 1960. (Huber bought the brand in 1995.) They also produce Blumer's Premium Sodas. On your tour you can sample both beverages. (*$, (608) 325-3191, huberbrewery.com*)

❻ **Madison Children's Museum:** This hands-on, interactive museum is designed primarily for young children and includes exhibits about everything from dinosaurs to gardens, dreams to your teeth and bones. Kids get to play while they learn and parents can participate, too. (*$, (608) 256-6445, madisonchildrensmuseum.com*)

Nighttime Fun

❶ **Blue Moon Bar:** This is a casual, neighborhood bar with two levels highlighted by architectural curves, pool and darts, TVs, and a jukebox that plays everything from Frank Sinatra to R.E.M. The menu features lots of sandwiches every day and lots of fish dishes on Fridays. (*$, (608) 233-0441, bluemoonbar.com*)

❷ **Capone's—The Bar Next Door:** In 1929 a Chicago gang that ran, among other "businesses," beer in large oil tanker trucks during Prohibition built this safehouse and underground bar with bullet-proof glass, bomb-proof walls, and round lookout rooms. Many of those features are still here, including the back bar, fireplace, and tunnel entrance (the other end of the tunnel was at a nearby lake for quick getaways). If you're wondering about the name, the gang that built the original bar was the group that supplied Al Capone with beer during Prohibition. (*$, (608) 256-9430, thecoliseumbar.com/index2.html*) ❸ **Cardinal Bar:** Often on Madison's

"Best of" lists for dance clubs, Cardinal offers a wide range of music to dance to from electronic to Latin, disco to funk, '80s to jazz. It also prides itself on bringing new urban, hip trends to Madison. This is a favorite for the college crowd and the just-out-of-college crowd. The full bar includes a pretty good selection of microbrews. (*$, (608) 251-0080, cardinalbar.com*) ❹ **The Great Dane:** *Madison Magazine* readers named this the "Best Brewpub" and "Best Microbrewery" in the city. This popular place to relax with a beer is located downtown in a restored hotel, livery, and eatery built during the 1850s and 1880s (the Victorian, cream-colored side of the building is the "newer" half). The bar also offers billiards and an antique humidor with premium cigars. The menu is brew pub fare, but the kitchen stays open until 1:00 a.m. serving from the late-night menu. There's also a second location in Fitchburg. (*$, (608) 284-0000, greatdanepub.com*) ❺ **Porta Bella:** On the main level is the Italian restaurant and wine bar that's been voted the "Best of Madison." Downstairs is the Cellar with its signature martini, wine, and microbrew menu. And it's downstairs where locals often relax and talk the night away. The Cellar menu has more

than 60 wines, scores of cocktails, and more than a dozen microbrews and imports on tap. If you're hungry, the menu upstairs, in the restaurant, has traditional Italian dishes alongside steak and seafood. (*$, (608) 256-3186, portabellarestaurant.biz*)

Shopping

❶ **Monroe Street:** This popular neighborhood near the university includes scores of shops to sell you everything from clothes to art to antiques. Several boutiques line the street, which also features green spaces. If you're hungry there are plenty of places to grab something to eat too.

❷ **State Street:** Running from the university to the state capitol, this popular street has a variety of shops selling most anything you would want. It also offers entertainment in the fashion of street performers. One highlight is the **House of Wisconsin Cheese,** which works with more than 60 Wisconsin dairies to stock a wide selection of one of the state's most famous products (you can buy it in the shape of the Wisconsin W and Bucky, too). There are also a lot of restaurants and bars so the area is busy day and night. (*state-st.com*) ❸ **The University Book Store:** Need something with Bucky or a W on it? You've found the place. The main store on campus has everything cardinal and white you'd expect, and a few things you might not, like Bucky Celebriduck—your favorite badger fashioned as a duck that squeaks and floats in the tub. Really. (*(800) 993-BOOK, uwbookstore.com*)

RECIPES

Breakfast Bites

Appetizers

Soups & Salads

Sides

Sweet Treats

Breakfast Bites

POTATOES LASKOWSKI CASSEROLE

Making potatoes easier to handle and easier to serve, this delicious casserole only needs heating up! This makes a hearty breakfast dish on cold mornings.

INGREDIENTS:
1 can cream of chicken soup
1 cup sour cream
¾ cup shredded cheddar cheese
½ medium onion, chopped
¼ cup melted butter
1 bag Potatoes O'Brien

DIRECTIONS:
Add everything except the potatoes and stir together until well combined. Add the potatoes and mix until incorporated. Cook in an aluminum steam tray pan for 45 minutes at 375°F. Let cool and package up for the tailgate. Heat up on a steam tray or Coleman stove when you're ready to serve this.

Yields 6 to 8 servings

Brent Laskowski, PennStateTailgate.com

BACONEGGANDCHEESE SANDWICHES

A must for the hungry breakfast tailgater. This sandwich is an American classic but tastes even better outdoors at your favorite sporting event. The keys are fresh cheese and a toaster for your Coleman stove.

INGREDIENTS:
1 pound sliced bacon
1 dozen fresh eggs
1 loaf white bread
12 slices deli American cheese

DIRECTIONS:
Use a Coleman Road Trip Grill (or similar portable grill) to fry the bacon. Set aside. Crack and fry 2 eggs. Use a wire camp toaster on a burner of your propane stove to prepare the toast, flipping until brown. Once eggs are prepared, place cheese on top and close lid of grill until melted. Top with 2 slices of bacon and serve to the next hungry tailgater!

Yields 6 to 12 servings

Jared Bean, PennStateTailgate.com

PECAN-CINNAMON COFFEE CAKE

FILLING INGREDIENTS:
1 ½ cups packed brown sugar
½ cup white sugar
2 teaspoons cinnamon
½ cup (1 stick) butter
1 ½ cups chopped pecans

CAKE INGREDIENTS:
1 cup (2 sticks) butter; softened
½ cup sugar
3 eggs
2 ½ cups flour
2 teaspoons baking powder
½ teaspoon salt
1 ½ cups sour cream
1 teaspoon vanilla extract

DIRECTIONS FOR FILLING:
Combine the brown sugar, white sugar, and cinnamon in a bowl and stir to mix well. Cut in the butter until crumbly. Stir in the pecans.

DIRECTIONS FOR CAKE:
Grease and flour a 9x13-inch cake pan. Cream the butter and sugar in a mixing bowl until light and fluffy. Add the eggs and mix well. Add the flour, baking powder, and salt and mix well. Stir in the sour cream and vanilla; the batter will be stiff. Spoon half of the cake batter evenly into the prepared pan. Sprinkle half of the filling over the batter. Repeat with

the remaining batter and filling. Bake at 350°F for 45 minutes or until a wooden pick inserted in the center comes out clean.

Yields 12 servings

Recipe from Always Superb: Recipes for Every Occasion, *courtesy of the Junior Leagues of Minneapolis & Saint Paul*

Appetizers

TAPENADE

INGREDIENTS:
1 pound calamata olives
1 can flat anchovies, including oil
2 large cloves of garlic
¼ to ⅓ cup capers, drained (use the big cheap ones in this recipe)
3 to 4 tablespoons chopped parsley
2 tablespoons lemon juice
¼ to ⅓ cup olive oil
French bread

DIRECTIONS:
Peel olive flesh from pits and discard pits. Combine olives, anchovies, garlic, capers, and parsley in blender or food processor. Blend, but retain some texture. Add lemon juice and olive oil to mixture. Blend in quickly. Spread on slices of French bread. Serve at room temperature.

Yields about 2 cups

Melissa Jacobi, Network and User Support Services, from Northwestern Library Staff Association Cookbook, *courtesy of the staff members at Northwestern Library*

BECKY'S WORLD FAMOUS CRACKER MIX

A staple on our tailgate menu from day one. This truly is a heart attack waiting to happen.

INGREDIENTS:
4 boxes of assorted crackers (Cheez-Its, Goldfish, pretzels, oyster crackers, etc.)
One packet of dry ranch dressing mix
1 bottle of popping corn oil

DIRECTIONS:
Mix all the crackers together with the ranch mix and popping corn oil (yes, the whole bottle) in a large bowl with a lid. Stir until evenly coated, then every so often until all the oil has been absorbed. Warning! This is highly addictive.

Yields 15 to 20 servings

Becky Grove, PennStateTailgate.com

HOT CHILI DIP

INGREDIENTS:
1 can of "no beans" chili
2 pounds Velveeta cheese
3 jalapeño peppers
1 medium onion, chopped

DIRECTIONS:
Put all ingredients in a bowl and microwave, mixing occasionally, until blended. Use as a dip for crackers or tortilla chips.

Yields about 3 ½ cups

Recipe from a-MAIZE-ing tailgating cookbook, *courtesy of Momentum Books, LLC*

PIGSKIN SHRIMP

These are simple to prepare for a tailgate.

INGREDIENTS:
Large precooked shrimp (as many as you want)
1 slice of bacon for every 3 shrimp
Barbecue sauce of your choosing
Skewers (as many as you need)

DIRECTIONS:
Cut slices of bacon into thirds. Wrap each shrimp with a piece of bacon and put on skewer. Repeat until skewers are stacked full. Place skewered shrimp on hot grill for about 3 minutes; turn and brush with barbecue sauce. Grill 3 minutes more, then turn and brush other side with barbecue sauce. Then grill a couple more minutes and remove. Note: It is best to use thinly sliced bacon as it crisps up quicker.

Tim Theisen, from Hawkeye Style *cookbook, courtesy of the Memphis Iowa Club*

CHICKEN SATAY WITH THREE SAUCES

PEANUT SAUCE INGREDIENTS:

8 ounces peanut butter

1 ½ teaspoons garlic powder

1 ½ teaspoons ground ginger

¼ teaspoon cayenne pepper

2 tablespoons soy sauce

2 tablespoons rice vinegar

¾ cup hot water

CARIBBEAN BARBECUE SAUCE INGREDIENTS:

1 red onion, chopped

4 garlic cloves

1 tablespoon freshly squeezed lime juice

1 tomato, chopped into ¼-inch pieces

4 cups tomato sauce

1 cup chili paste

Dash of pepper

CURRY SAUCE INGREDIENTS:

2 roasted red peppers, peeled and seeded

4 ½ ounces gingerroot, sliced

9 garlic cloves

½ cup chili paste

2 tablespoons curry powder

2 teaspoons cardamom

2 teaspoons salt

3 (10-ounce) cans coconut milk

CHICKEN SATAY INGREDIENTS:
6 or more boneless, skinless chicken breasts
Bamboo skewers

PEANUT SAUCE DIRECTIONS:
Whisk the peanut butter, garlic powder, ginger, cayenne pepper, soy sauce, and vinegar together in a bowl. Whisk in the water gradually.

BARBECUE SAUCE DIRECTIONS:
Coarsely puree the onion, garlic, and lime juice in a food processor. Pour into a bowl. Add the tomato, tomato sauce, chili paste, and pepper and mix well.

CURRY SAUCE DIRECTIONS:
Puree the red peppers, gingerroot, garlic, chili paste, curry powder, cardamom, and salt in a food processor. Add the coconut milk and mix well.

SATAY DIRECTIONS:
Cut the chicken into bite size pieces. Thread 4 to 6 pieces of chicken on a water-soaked bamboo skewer. Repeat with the remaining chicken. Place on a grill rack. Grill over hot coals for 8 to 10 minutes or until the chicken is cooked through. Serve with the sauces.

Yields 6 or more servings

Recipe from Always Superb: Recipes for Every Occasion, *courtesy of the Junior Leagues of Minneapolis & Saint Paul.*

LAYERED ASIAN APPETIZER DIP

ZIPPY SWEET-AND-SOUR SAUCE INGREDIENTS:

¼ cup packed brown sugar

2 teaspoons cornstarch

1 cup water

¼ cup ketchup

2 tablespoons vinegar

1 tablespoon Worcestershire sauce

3 drops of hot red pepper sauce

TOPPING INGREDIENTS:

¼ cup chopped cooked chicken

½ cup finely shredded carrot

¼ cup chopped unsalted peanuts

3 tablespoons sliced scallions

1 tablespoon chopped fresh parsley

2 teaspoons soy sauce

¼ teaspoon ground ginger or 1 teaspoon grated gingerroot

BASE INGREDIENTS:

8 ounces cream cheese, softened

1 tablespoon milk

DIRECTIONS FOR THE SAUCE:

Combine the brown sugar and cornstarch in a small saucepan and mix well. Stir in the water, ketchup, vinegar, Worcestershire sauce and hot sauce gradually. Cook over medium heat for 5 minutes or until the mixture thickens slightly, stirring frequently. Let stand until cool. Chill, covered until ready to use; this will thicken in the refrigerator.

DIRECTIONS FOR TOPPING:

Combine the chicken, carrot, peanuts, scallions, parsley, soy sauce, ginger and garlic in a bowl and mix well. Chill, covered, for 8 to 12 hours.

DIRECTIONS FOR BASE:
Combine the cream cheese and milk in a mixing bowl. Beat until smooth and fluffy.

To Assemble: Spread the base mixture over the bottom of a 10-inch round serving dish. Spoon the topping evenly over the base. Drizzle with ½ cup of the sauce, reserving the remaining sauce for another use. Serve with table water crackers and other assorted crackers.

You may double the base and topping recipes and use a larger dish.

Yields 10 to 12 servings

Recipe from Always Superb: Recipes for Every Occasion *provided courtesy of the Junior Leagues of Minneapolis & Saint Paul.*

ARTICHOKE SPREAD

INGREDIENTS:
1 can artichoke hearts, chopped
1 cup Parmesan cheese
1 cup mayonnaise
Dash of garlic powder
Dash of lemon juice

DIRECTIONS:
Mix and bake at 350°F until browned. Serve with crusty French bread.

Yields about 3 cups

Peter Devlin, Catalog, from Northwestern Library Staff Association Cookbook, *courtesy of the staff members at Northwestern Library*

SPINACH DIP

A delicious snack for the tailgate. It also adds vegetables you usually don't serve at a sporting event.

INGREDIENTS:
1 packet instant vegetable soup mix (like Knorr or Mrs. Grass)
1 pint sour cream
¾ cup mayo
6 ounces frozen spinach, drained, thawed, and chopped
2 green onions, chopped
1 can water chestnuts, drained
1 round, crusty loaf of bread

DIRECTIONS:
Mix together first 6 ingredients. Let dip sit in the fridge or cooler for 1 to 2 hours (or overnight) before serving. At the tailgate party, take a sharp serrated knife and cut a round hole in the top of the bread. Remove top and scoop out bread from inside loaf, being careful not to puncture bottom. Save the removed bread. Pour dip into the hollowed out loaf and serve with saved bread and cut veggies.

Yields about 6 cups

Heather Bean, PennStateTailgate.com

JERKED WINGS

This one is a little more involved but can be prepared ahead of time. It has been a staple at the Memphis Iowa Club tailgates when we travel back to Iowa City.

INGREDIENTS:
15 chicken wings
¼ teaspoon black pepper
½ cup onion
¼ teaspoon curry powder.
2 tablespoons lime juice
¼ teaspoon thyme
1 teaspoon salt
⅛ teaspoon ground red pepper
1 teaspoon crushed red pepper
⅛ teaspoon ground ginger
½ teaspoon allspice
2 cloves garlic minced

DIRECTIONS:
Mix all ingredients except wings in blender. Put wings in 1-gallon Ziploc bag and pour in mixture. Marinate 4 hours, or overnight, and then place on hot grill. Cook until juices run clear when pierced. These are especially good on a cool fall day.

Yields 15 wings, or 5 servings

Tim Theisen from Hawkeye Style *cookbook, courtesy of the Memphis Iowa Club*

COUNTRY PATÉ

INGREDIENTS:
1 package bacon slices
1 pound chicken livers
1 pound sausage meat
Salt and pepper
¼ teaspoon thyme
1 cup dry sherry
3 or 4 bay leaves

DIRECTIONS:
Preheat oven to 400°F. Line 1 oblong baking dish (Pyrex or similar) preferably with cover with bacon slices, leaving ends to wrap over paté. In food processor or blender, grind raw chicken livers. Mix with sausage meat, salt and pepper, and thyme, blending until smooth. Pour into bacon-lined baking dish. Pour sherry over mixture; fold bacon slices over top of mixture. Place bay leaves on top. Cover, and/or wrap entire dish tightly in several thicknesses of aluminum foil. Place on cookie sheet. Bake 2 hours. Turn oven off and let paté sit in oven 2 or 3 hours longer. Remove from oven and refrigerate. When ready to serve, remove fat around paté and unmold. Serve with cocktail rye, crackers, or French bread.

Yields 1 loaf of paté

Jacqueline Gelso, Catalog, from Northwestern Library Staff Association Cookbook, *courtesy of the staff members at Northwestern Library*

GAZEBO K-BOBS

Meat on a stick. Who could ask for anything more? Just put your favorite meat on a stick and impress everyone at your tailgate party.

INGREDIENTS:
3 to 4 pounds beef, chicken, or pork
1 bottle of Gazebo Room Greek Salad Dressing & Marinade (available at local groceries)
Wooden skewers

DIRECTIONS:
Cut meat into 1-inch squares and place on skewers. Place in a plastic container and marinate in Gazebo dressing overnight. Grill to perfection and serve hot. The crowd will be begging for more. Bring plenty because these babies are always popular with hungry tailgaters.

Yields 6 to 8 servings

Recipe courtesy of gazeboroom.com and PennStateTailgate.com

FRUIT SALAD

INGREDIENTS:
1 package vanilla pudding
1 package vanilla tapioca pudding
1 can Mandarin oranges
1 can pineapple chunks
1 heaping tablespoon of frozen concentrated orange juice
Fresh blueberries

DIRECTIONS:
Cook puddings together with 3 cups liquid (use liquids from canned fruits
with orange juice concentrate and add water to make your 3 cups). Cook
slightly, and then add Mandarin oranges and pineapple chunks.
Refrigerate overnight. Before serving, sprinkle with fresh blueberries for
Illini colors—orange and blue.

Yields 6 to 8 servings

Corinne Brown, from From Tailgates Through Celebrations *cookbook, courtesy of
University of Illinois Mothers Association*

TANGY BROCCOLI SALAD

INGREDIENTS:
1 cup Miracle Whip, or Miracle Whip Lite salad dressing
2 tablespoons sugar
2 tablespoons vinegar
1 medium bunch broccoli, cut into flowerets
4 cups loosely packed fresh spinach leaves
8 ounces bacon, crisply cooked and crumbled
½ cup red onion, cut into strips
¼ cup raisins

DIRECTIONS:
Mix dressing, sugar, and vinegar in a large bowl. Add remaining ingredients, mix lightly. Refrigerate.

Yields 8 servings

Recipe from a-MAIZE-ing tailgating cookbook, *courtesy of Momentum Books, LLC*

AVOCADO CORN CONFETTI SALAD

INGREDIENTS:
3 avocados
3 (11-ounce) cans Shoe Peg white corn, drained
1 red bell pepper, chopped
1 red onion, chopped, or 6 green onions, chopped
¼ cup olive oil
⅔ cup red wine vinegar
2 teaspoons red pepper
2 teaspoons oregano
Juice of 3 or 4 limes

DIRECTIONS:
Peel and chop the avocados. Combine with the corn, bell pepper, and onion in a bowl mix well. Combine the olive oil, vinegar, red pepper, oregano, and lime juice in a separate bowl and mix well. Pour over the salad. Serve this as an appetizer with corn chips.

Yields 6 to 8 servings

Recipe from Always Superb: Recipes for Every Occasion, *courtesy of the Junior Leagues of Minneapolis & Saint Paul*

CORN CHOWDER

INGREDIENTS:
4 cups corn, cut from cob (about 8 large ears) divided
1 tablespoon margarine
2 cups chopped onion
1 cup diced celery
2 ounces diced, lower-salt deli ham
2 cloves garlic, minced
2 ½ cups peeled, diced baking potatoes (about 1 ¼ lbs)
2 (10 ½ ounce) cans low-sodium chicken broth
¼ cup plus 2 tablespoons all-purpose flour
½ teaspoon salt
¼ teaspoon black pepper
⅛ teaspoon ground red pepper
2 cups 2 % milk
1 teaspoon Worcestershire

DIRECTIONS:
Position knife blade in food processor bowl; add 2 ½ cups corn. Process until smooth; set aside. Melt margarine in a large Dutch oven over medium heat. Add onion and next 3 ingredients and sauté 10 minutes, or until vegetables are tender, stirring occasionally. Add potato and broth; bring to a boil. Reduce heat and simmer, uncovered, 20 minutes or until potatoes are tender, stirring frequently. Add the corn puree and remaining 1 ½ cups corn. Cook 10 minutes. Place flour and next 3 ingredients in a small bowl. Gradually add milk and Worcestershire, blending with a wire whisk; add to chowder. Cook over medium heat or until thickened, stirring constantly.

Yields 6 to 8 servings

Recipe from a-MAIZE-ing tailgating cookbook, *courtesy of Momentum Books, LLC*

Sides

CAJUN "DIRTY" RICE

INGREDIENTS:
1 pound chicken gizzards, finely chopped
1 pound chicken livers, finely chopped
¼ cup squeeze Parkay Margarine
1 ½ cups finely chopped onion
½ cup finely chopped celery
½ cup finely chopped green pepper
2 garlic cloves minced
2 teaspoons salt
1 teaspoon pepper
⅛ teaspoon ground red pepper
3 cups hot cooked Minute Rice
½ cup chopped parsley

DIRECTIONS:
Brown meat in margarine in a large skillet. Add onion, celery, green pepper, garlic, and seasonings; mix well. Cover. Cook over medium heat, stirring occasionally, until vegetables are tender. Add rice and parsley; mix lightly. Serve immediately.

Yields 8 servings

Vicky Morgan, Acquisitions, from Northwestern Library Staff Association Cookbook, *courtesy of the staff members at Northwestern Library*

GRILLED POTATOES

INGREDIENTS:
⅓ cup Miracle Whip salad dressing
3 garlic cloves, minced
½ teaspoon paprika
¼ teaspoon salt
¼ teaspoon pepper
3 baking potatoes cut into ¼-inch slices
1 large onion, red or white

DIRECTIONS:
Mix salad dressing and seasonings in large bowl until well blended.
Stir in potatoes and onions to coat. Divide potato mixture evenly among
12-inch squares of heavy-duty aluminum foil. Seal each to form a packet.
Place foil packets on grill over medium-hot coals. Grill 25 to 30 minutes,
or until tender.

Yields 6 servings

Monica Janicki from From Tailgates Through Celebrations *cookbook, courtesy of
University of Illinois Mothers Association*

MIXED GRILL VEGETABLES

This easy recipe appeals to those health conscious tailgaters who don't want to get too weighed down to enjoy the game. Just add your favorites, and this recipe can serve as little or as many as you want and is great for outdoor, easy cooking.

INGREDIENTS:
5 green bell peppers
3 large Vidalia onion
5 yellow squash
1 (2-pound) package grape tomatoes
Other vegetables
Kosher salt and pepper to taste
1 bottle Gazebo Room Greek Salad Dressing & Marinade (available at local groceries)

DIRECTIONS:
Cut assorted fresh vegetables in large chunks. Put cut vegetables in a large bowl and season with kosher salt and fresh ground pepper. Add Gazebo Room Marinade. Stir to coat and place on a hot grill pan or skillet if you don't have one. Cook until tender and place back in the bowl used to coat vegetables to give added flavor. Use as many vegetables as desired. Serve immediately.

Yields 6 to 8 servings

Brent Laskowski, PennStateTailgate.com

KUGELIS

INGREDIENTS:
5 pounds Idaho potatoes
2 large onions
6 eggs, beaten
1 cup (2 sticks) butter, melted
¼ pound bacon
Dairy sour cream

DIRECTIONS:
Preheat oven to 350°F. Grease a 9x13-inch baking pan; set aside. Peel and grate potatoes and onions. (Do not use a blender for grating—use the fine side of a hand grater.) Combine grated potatoes and onions in a mixing bowl; add eggs and butter and mix well. Spread mixture in prepared pan. Bake at 350°F for 1 ½ hours to 2 hours or until golden brown. While kugelis is baking, fry bacon until crisp; drain and crumble. Cut warm kugelis into squares to serve; top each serving with a dollop of sour cream and a sprinkle of bacon. Bake this a day ahead of time and then refrigerate it. At your tailgate party, place a sheet of heavy duty aluminum foil on your grill and spray lightly with nonstick cooking spray. Place the kugelis on the foil to reheat, turning once.

Yields 8 to 12 servings

Recipes from The Michigan State University Experience, *courtesy of author* Bob Bao

Main Dishes

GRILLED ROSEMARY CHICKEN

INGREDIENTS:
2 broiler chickens (3 pounds each)
1 large clove garlic
½ cup olive oil
2 tablespoons fresh lemon juice
2 tablespoons balsamic or red wine vinegar
1 ½ tablespoons Worcestershire sauce
1 tablespoon dried rosemary
2 teaspoons Dijon mustard
1 teaspoon salt
1 teaspoon dried basil
1 teaspoon crushed red pepper

DIRECTIONS:
Prepare charcoal fire or preheat grill. Combine all ingredients except chicken in a small dish; mix well. Transfer to a large plastic food bag. Add chicken and seal bag. Turn bag over several times until chicken is well coated. Refrigerate 2 to 4 hours. Grill chicken over heat source, turning once, until juices run clear—about 15 minutes. If chicken is thicker it may take more time. Serve hot or at room temperature.

Jackie Buckley, from From Tailgates Through Celebrations *cookbook, courtesy of University of Illinois Mothers Association*

OLIVE BURGER

INGREDIENTS:
1 jar (12 ounces) green olives stuffed with pimentos, drained well
   and sliced
1 cup mayonnaise
2 teaspoons sugar
½ teaspoon lemon juice
1 ⅓ pounds ground beef
4 hamburger buns
Garnish: Dill pickles

DIRECTIONS:
In a medium mixing bowl, combine olives, mayonnaise, sugar, and lemon juice; mix well. Cover and refrigerate until thoroughly chilled.

Form ground beef into 4 ⅓-pound burgers. Cook burgers to desired doneness on grill. Place each burger on the bottom half of a bun, then top with a large scoop of olive mixture. Serve sandwich open-faced, with the top of the bun on the side. Garnish with a dill pickle.

Yields 4 servings

Recipes from The Michigan State University Experience, *courtesy of author Bob Bao*

STROMBOLI SANDWICH

INGREDIENTS:

1 pound mild Italian sausage, casings removed

8 ounces ground beef

1 cup chopped green bell pepper

1 cup chopped onion

1 cup sliced fresh mushrooms

1 (8-ounce) can tomato sauce

1 (6-ounce) can tomato paste

¼ cup water

¼ cup (1-ounce) grated Parmesan cheese

¼ teaspoon oregano

¼ teaspoon rosemary

¼ teaspoon salt

1 (1 ½ pound) loaf Vienna bread

3 cups (12 ounces) shredded mozzarella cheese

DIRECTIONS:

Brown the sausage and ground beef in a skillet, stirring until crumbly; drain. Add the bell pepper, onion, and mushrooms. Sauté for 5 minutes. Stir the tomato sauce, tomato paste, water, Parmesan cheese, oregano, rosemary, and salt into the sausage mixture. Bring to a simmer. Simmer for 10 minutes stirring occasionally. Cut the bread into halves lengthwise. Scoop out the centers to form bread shells, reserving the bread centers for another use. Layer half of the mozzarella cheese, sausage mixture, and remaining mozzarella cheese in the bottom shell. Wrap in foil. Bake at 400°F, or place on a hot grill for 6 to 8 minutes until heated through. Slice and serve.

Yields 6 to 8 servings

Recipe from Always Superb: Recipes for Every Occasion, *courtesy of the Junior Leagues of Minneapolis & Saint Paul*

HOAGIES

INGREDIENTS:
2 long loaves French bread
Lettuce, chopped
Tomatoes, sliced
Onions, sliced thin
Avocado, sliced (optional)
Italian salad dressing
Garlic salt
1 to ½ pounds spiced ham, shaved
½ pound Genoa salami, sliced thin
½ pound mozzarella or provolone cheese, sliced thin

DIRECTIONS:
Cut loaves of bread lengthwise, cutting ¾ of the way through loaf. Open loaves, cut side up. Line with chopped lettuce. Layer on tomatoes, onion, and avocado. In a small bowl, mix salad dressing with garlic salt to taste, then sprinkle over vegetable layers. Next, layer meats and cheese, then fold loaf over. For vegetarians, omit meats and add more vegetables and cheese. Wrap loaf sandwich and take to your tailgate party, where your family and guests can cut off the portion size they each want.

Yields 10 to 12 servings

Nancy Rotzoll, from From Tailgates Through Celebrations *cookbook, courtesy of University of Illinois Mothers Association*

TY'S RIBS

INGREDIENTS:
1 rack loin back ribs (per 2 people)
1 tablespoon Hawkeye Ty's Dry Rub & Seasoning, per rack (page 201)
2 cups of barbecue BBQ Baste, per rack (page 201)
6 cups hickory chips soaked in water

DIRECTIONS:
Start by pulling membrane from back of each rack of ribs. Season generously with dry rub. Place directly over coals on grill for about 15 to 20 minutes per side until lightly browned. Then move to edge of heat source and baste. Also add wet hickory chips to hot coals at this time. If your grill isn't big enough to handle all the ribs, you can cook directly over coals by rotating racks every 30 minutes and keeping the heat low. Add a few coals as necessary to keep heat up. Cook for 4 to 5 hours. You can usually tell if they're done by bending the rack; if it starts to come apart, they're done.

There are several ways to serve ribs: you can sprinkle generously with dry rub just before serving or slather with sauce just before serving. You may also brush with sauce during the final 30 minutes of grilling. Just be careful—the sauce burns easily. Note: Always make an extra rack to snack on later, around midnight or so.

Yields 2 servings per rack

Tim Theisen, from Hawkeye Style *cookbook, courtesy of the Memphis Iowa Club*

HAWKEYE TY'S DRY RUB & SEASONING

INGREDIENTS:

¼ cup paprika

2 teaspoons salt

¾ teaspoon black pepper

¾ teaspoon white pepper

¼ teaspoon red pepper

½ teaspoon ground mustard

1 teaspoon onion powder

1 tablespoon chili powder

½ teaspoon crushed coriander

½ teaspoon crushed rosemary

1 teaspoon mustard seed

DIRECTIONS:

Mix all ingredients together. Rub on meat before cooking or sprinkle on afterward.

BBQ BASTE

INGREDIENTS:

1 egg

½ cup vegetable oil

1 cup cider vinegar

1 tablespoon salt

1 teaspoon dry rub (above)

DIRECTIONS:

Whisk egg and oil together, then mix in vinegar and seasonings.

Yields about 2 cups

Tim Theisen, from Hawkeye Style *cookbook, courtesy of the Memphis Iowa Club*

LONDON BROIL

INGREDIENTS:
3 to 4 pounds London Broil steak
1 small onion, chopped
4 tablespoons vinegar
½ cup ketchup
2 tablespoons brown sugar
4 tablespoons salad oil
2 teaspoons salt
1 teaspoon Tabasco

DIRECTIONS:
Place meat and onion in shallow glass dish. Combine rest of ingredients and mix well. Pour over meat and turn. Cover dish with foil and marinate 12 to 24 hours in refrigerator. Remove meat from sauce and cook on medium to hot barbecue grill no longer than 10 to 15 minutes per side. Brush occasionally with sauce. Slice thin, on a diagonal. Meat should be juicy and pink in the center.

Yields 4 to 6 servings

Will and Marlys Smith, from Hawkeye Style *cookbook, courtesy of the Memphis Iowa Club*

PIZZA CASSEROLE

A delicious alternative to traditional tailgate food, this is a casserole you can prepare at home the week before and heat up at the stadium. One of our most popular dishes.

INGREDIENTS:
1 pound ground beef
2 cups rotini pasta
2 (16-ounce) jars of Del Grosso pepperoni-flavored pizza sauce
2 to 3 cups mozzarella
Pepperoni, if desired

DIRECTIONS:
Brown beef and drain. Cook noodles and drain. Combine beef, noodles, and sauce in 2-quart aluminum disposable baking pan. Sprinkle mozzarella cheese on top. Top with pepperoni if desired. Heat on a grill or steam table for 1 hour, or until cheese is completely melted.

Yields 6 to 8 servings

Diane Harris, PennStateTailgate.com

SPICY MARINATED FLANK STEAK

INGREDIENTS:
2 flank steaks
1 ½ cups vegetable oil
¾ cup soy sauce
½ cup wine vinegar
⅓ cup lemon juice
2 or 3 garlic cloves, crushed
¼ cup Worcestershire sauce
2 tablespoons dry mustard
2 teaspoons salt
1 teaspoon pepper
2 or 3 garlic cloves, crushed

DIRECTIONS:
Score the steaks in a diamond pattern with a sharp knife. Place in a deep dish. Combine the vegetable oil, soy sauce, wine vinegar, lemon juice, crushed garlic, Worcestershire sauce, dry mustard, salt, and pepper in a bowl and mix well. Pour over the steaks. Marinate, covered, in the refrigerator for 8 hours or longer. Drain steaks, discarding the marinade. Place on a grill rack and grill over hot coals until steak has reached the desired degree of doneness. Cut the steaks across the grain into thin slices to serve.

Yields 8 to 10 servings

Recipe from America Celebrates Columbus *cookbook, courtesy of the Junior League of Columbus*

TY'S TENDERLOINS

This is a thick slice of pork loin pounded and breaded and deep fried. This sandwich is very unique to this part of the country. Having been gone from the area for some years now I'm really not familiar with the best place to order one, but I've been told that Jonesy's in Solon, Iowa, serves up one of the best. If people visiting the Iowa City area don't have the means to make one they should definitely find a place like Jonesy's to sample one.

INGREDIENTS:
Oil for deep frying
1 pork loin, sliced ¾ to 1 inch thick
Salt
Pepper
Garlic salt
2 eggs
¼ cup milk
1 sleeve Saltine crackers, finely crushed

DIRECTIONS:
Heat oil to 375°F. Pound pork loin to desired thickness. (Some like it very thin, I prefer about ⅜ to ½ inch thick.) Season with salt, pepper, and garlic salt. Combine egg and milk and whisk. Dip pork loin in egg mixture and roll in cracker crumbs. Carefully drop into deep fryer for 3 to 4 minutes. Serve on a hamburger bun with favorite condiments.

Yields 8 to 10 servings

Tim Theisen from Hawkeye Style *cookbook, courtesy of the Memphis Iowa Club*

BEGGAR'S HOT BEEF CHILI

INGREDIENTS:
8 pounds beef stew meat
12 cups coarsely chopped onions
6 cups chopped jalapeños
5 cans (12 ½ cups each) tomatoes
1 quart cider vinegar
¾ cup finely chopped garlic
½ cup dried oregano leaves
½ cup ground cumin seed
5 cans (12 ½ cups each) kidney beans

DIRECTIONS:
Combine all ingredients except kidney beans in a 10-gallon pot; mix well.
Bring to a boil, then reduce heat to low. Cover pot and simmer, stirring
frequently for 3 to 4 hours or until the meat is very tender. Add beans and
simmer another hour.

Yields about 50 servings

For 14 to 16 servings, the above quantities can be reduced to the
following amounts:
2 pounds beef stew meat
3 cups coarsely chopped onions
1 ½ cups jalapeños
2 (14-ounce) cans tomatoes
½ cup cider vinegar
3 tablespoons finely chopped garlic
2 tablespoons dried oregano leaves
2 tablespoons ground cumin seed
2 (14-ounce) cans kidney beans

Recipes from The Michigan State University Experience, *courtesy of author Bob Bao*

FLAME'S HOT SPICY CHICKEN BARBECUE

INGREDIENTS:
½ cup A-1 Steak Sauce
½ cup tomato sauce
¼ cup finely chopped onion
2 teaspoons cider vinegar
2 teaspoons maple syrup
1 teaspoon vegetable oil
3 teaspoons chili powder
½ teaspoon crushed red pepper flakes
1 (3-pound) chicken, cut up

DIRECTIONS:
In a medium saucepan, combine steak sauce, tomato sauce, onion, vinegar, maple syrup, oil, chili powder, and red pepper flakes. Over medium heat, heat to a boil; then reduce heat. Simmer 5 to 7 minutes or until thickened. Cool. Grill chicken over medium heat 30 to 40 minutes, or until done, turning and basting frequently with prepared sauce. Serve hot.

Yields 4 to 6 servings

Recipes from a-MAIZE-ing tailgating cookbook, *courtesy of Momentum Books, LLC*

DEEP FRIED TURKEY

INGREDIENTS:
1 (12 to 15 pound) turkey
1 pound margarine
2 ounces garlic juice
2 ounces onion juice
5 tablespoons Tony Chachere's Creole Seasoning
1 teaspoon cayenne pepper
Worcestershire sauce
Peanut oil

DIRECTIONS:
Remove all excess parts from turkey (neck bones, gizzard, auto-thermometer); rinse well and pat dry. In saucepan, melt margarine and add garlic juice, onion juice, and Tony Chachere's seasoning. Add cayenne pepper and Worcestershire to taste. Inject turkey. (There is enough to inject two turkeys.) Refrigerate overnight. Heat peanut oil in turkey fryer pot to 375°F. Slowly lower turkey into pot and deep fry at 350°F for 3 to 3 ½ minutes per pound. Note: It's wise to use the deep fryer pot when rinsing the turkey the day before. Put the turkey in the pot and just cover with water. Remove turkey and mark the water's level. This gives you an accurate way to measure the amount of oil you need in the pot.

Yields 8 to 10 servings

Tim Theisen, from Hawkeye Style *cookbook, courtesy of the Memphis Iowa Club*

GRILLED HERB & GARLIC FISH

INGREDIENTS:
½ cup mayonnaise, or mayonnaise-type salad dressing
½ teaspoon dried marjoram leaves
½ teaspoon dried thyme leaves
½ teaspoon garlic powder
¼ teaspoon ground celery seed
1 pound grouper, flounder, mahi-mahi or swordfish fillets

DIRECTIONS:
Combine the mayonnaise, marjoram, thyme, garlic powder, and celery seed in a bowl and mix well. Place the fish on an oiled grill rack. Brush fish with half of the mayonnaise mixture. Grill over medium-hot coals for 5 to 8 minutes. Turn fish over. Brush with the remaining mayonnaise mixture. Grill for 5 to 8 minutes longer or until the fish flakes easily with a fork.

Yields 2 to 4 servings

Recipe from America Celebrates Columbus *cookbook, courtesy of the Junior League of Columbus*

PEPPER-MAN

INGREDIENTS:

1 pound ground chuck

2 teaspoons garlic salt

3 teaspoons oregano leaves

2 cups cooked rice (preferably fried rice for flavor, Rice-Roni chicken or
vegetable will suffice)

2 small cans of Hunts tomato sauce

2 tablespoons maple syrup (preferably Mrs. Butterworth's)

1 cup of Coca-Cola or Pepsi (can add a little more for thinner texture after
all ingredients are mixed)

1 to 2 cups of plump juicy raisins (depending on your gastrointestinal tract)

4 medium-size yellow peppers (red or green peppers may be substituted)

4 tablespoons of Parmesan cheese

DIRECTIONS:

Mix ground chuck, garlic salt, and oregano in saucepan and brown. Drain
excess fat. Leave somewhat chunky for hearty eaters. In a separate
saucepan mix fried rice, Hunts tomato sauce, syrup, Coca-Cola, and
raisins. Add ground chuck and mix. Cut a circle opening around the tops of
the peppers, just large enough for stuffing and to allow you to discard the
seeds. Stuff uncooked peppers with rice mixture and sit in a saucepan just
large enough for peppers to stand erect. Add 2 cups of water to saucepan
and bring to a boil. Cover peppers to get a steaming effect. Reduce heat
and let peppers stand in hot water no more than 5 minutes. Wrap in foil
to keep warm until serving. Add Parmesan cheese on top when serving.

Yields 4 servings

Charles Williams, Catalog, from Northwestern Library Staff Association
Cookbook, *courtesy of the staff members at Northwestern Library*

BEER B-Q

INGREDIENTS:
3 to 4 pounds beef brisket (fresh)
1 onion, chopped
1 bottle ketchup
1 can beer
Salt and pepper to taste

DIRECTIONS:
Put beef brisket in Dutch oven (or heavy pot) with the onion, ketchup, beer, salt, and pepper. Simmer 3 ½ hours at 350°F. Chill and refrigerate overnight. Slice meat thin the next day. Place in 9x13-inch dish and reheat in same sauce for 20 to 30 minutes. You can cook a larger brisket using the same amount of sauce. You can also freeze between the cooking and the slicing stages. Serve on buns or with noodles.

Yields 8 to 10 servings

Connie Avildsen, Transportation Library, from Northwestern Library Staff Association Cookbook, *courtesy of the staff members at Northwestern Library*

MEATBALL SANDWICH

MEATBALL INGREDIENTS:
2 pounds ground beef
7 ounces bread crumbs
½ tablespoon pepper
½ cup Parmesan cheese
1 ½ tablespoons chopped parsley
6 large eggs
¼ to ½ cup water
1 ½ tablespoons salt
1 ½ small to medium onions, chopped
1 teaspoon sugar
4 to 5 cloves garlic, finely chopped
Cooking oil

DIRECTIONS:
Mix ingredients except oil and roll into balls slightly larger than golf balls.
Brown meatballs in oil and place in tomato sauce. Cook in sauce for 30
minutes on medium heat or 1 hour on simmer. Let cool and cut meatballs
in half. You can freeze meatballs and sauce until game day. Heat at
tailgate and serve on small sub rolls. Cover with tomato sauce and
sprinkle with Parmesan or mozzarella cheese.

Yields about 50 meatballs

TOMATO SAUCE INGREDIENTS:
2 cloves chopped garlic
½ onion
Cooking oil
8 ounces tomato paste

2 cans tomato juice
1 can water
1 tablespoon sugar
½ tablespoon pepper
1 teaspoon parsley
1 teaspoon sweet basil
1 teaspoon oregano
2 bay leaves

OPTIONAL INGREDIENTS:
Mushrooms
Italian sausage
Wine
More or less garlic, pepper, and spices

DIRECTIONS FOR SAUCE:
Fry garlic and onion in oil until oil turns golden. Fry tomato paste. Add tomato juice and water. Add remaining ingredients.

Yields about 5 ⅓ cups sauce

Recipes from a-MAIZE-ing tailgating cookbook,
courtesy of Momentum Books, LLC

CREOLE STEW

INGREDIENTS:
½ cup olive oil
2 ribs celery, finely chopped
2 Vidalia onions, finely chopped
2 sweet green peppers, julienned
2 sweet red peppers, julienned
2 bay leaves
1 tablespoon Creole seasoning (or to taste)
1 teaspoon dried thyme leaves
1 pound precooked andouille sausage, cut into 2-inch pieces
1 pound boneless, skinless chicken breasts, grilled and cut into strips
1 pound cooked shrimp (30–40 count) tail on
4 large, very ripe tomatoes, cut into wedges
3 or 4 splashes hot pepper sauce or Tabasco (or to taste)
Salt and pepper
2 ears sweet corn, cut into 1-inch pieces (optional)
1 small package frozen cut okra
Water or V-8 juice, if needed
Hot cooked rice or orzo

DIRECTIONS:
Heat oil in a Dutch oven or large skillet, set over medium-high heat. Add celery, onions, green and red peppers, bay leaves, Creole seasoning, and thyme; sauté, stirring often, for about 3 to 5 minutes or until onions are transparent. Add sausage and chicken; cook, stirring often, for about 3 to 5 minutes or until sausage is lightly browned. Add shrimp, tomatoes, hot pepper sauce or Tabasco, salt, pepper, and corn, if desired; continue cooking, stirring constantly, for 2 to 3 minutes. Add okra and a splash of water or V-8 juice if the mixture looks too dry. Reduce heat, cover pan,

and simmer for 3 to 4 minutes. Serve over rice ("dirty" rice is best) or orzo, with a selection of hot sauces on the side.

Yields 6 to 8 servings

Recipes from The Michigan State University Experience, *courtesy of author Bob Bao*

Sweet Treats

ILLINI BARS

INGREDIENTS:
1 box German chocolate cake mix
⅔ cup sweetened condensed milk
¾ cup melted margarine
1 (14-ounce) bag caramels
1 (12-ounce) bag semisweet chocolate chips or milk chocolate chips

DIRECTIONS:
In a large mixing bowl, combine cake mix, ⅓ cup condensed milk, and margarine. Mix well. Spread half of dough into greased 9x13-inch pan. Bake at 350°F for 6 to 8 minutes. Melt caramels over low heat with remaining ⅓ cup condensed milk. Stir frequently. Sprinkle chocolate chips over first baked layer of cake. Pour caramel mixture over chips. Crumble remaining cake dough over all. Bake at 350°F for 15 to 18 minutes more. Cool before serving. May be frozen.

Yields 24 bars

Carol Berg from From Tailgates Through Celebrations *cookbook, courtesy of University of Illinois Mothers Association*

RUM CAKE

CAKE INGREDIENTS:
½ cup finely chopped pecans
1 (2-layer) yellow cake mix
1 (4-ounce) package vanilla instant pudding mix
½ cup light rum
½ cup water
½ cup vegetable oil
4 eggs

GLAZE INGREDIENTS:
¼ cup light rum
¼ cup water
1 cup sugar
½ cup (1 stick) butter
Pecans

CAKE DIRECTIONS:
Spray a bundt pan with nonstick cooking spray. Sprinkle the pecans over the bottom of the pan. Combine the cake mix, pudding mix, rum, water, oil, and eggs in a mixing bowl. Beat for 2 minutes. Pour into the prepared pan. Bake at 325°F for 50 minutes.

GLAZE DIRECTIONS:
Combine the rum, water, sugar, and butter in a saucepan. Bring to a boil. Boil for 2 minutes.

TO ASSEMBLE:
Pour half of the glaze over the warm cake in the pan. Let stand for 10 minutes. Invert onto a cake plate. Pour the remaining glaze over the cake. Garnish with pecans.

Yields 16 servings

Recipe from Always Superb: Recipes for Every Occasion, *provided courtesy of the Junior Leagues of Minneapolis & Saint Paul.*

FOURTH DOWN & BUNDT CAKE

INGREDIENTS:
1 box devil's food cake mix
1 ½ cups sour cream
¾ cup vegetable oil
½ cup Kahlúa
2 eggs (beat with fork)
1 (3.4-ounce) package instant vanilla pudding
Powdered sugar

DIRECTIONS:
Mix all together first 6 ingredients with a big spoon and leave lumpy. Bake at 350°F in a greased and floured bundt cake pan for 45 minutes. Cool. Dust top with powdered sugar. This recipe makes a very rich, moist cake. This isn't messy, so no forks or plates are needed. Easy!

Yields 12 servings

Recipes from a-MAIZE-ing tailgating *cookbook, courtesy of Momentum Books, LLC*

CHOCOLATE SOUR CREAM FUDGE CAKE

INGREDIENTS:

2 cups flour

2 teaspoons baking soda

½ teaspoon salt

2 ¼ cups packed light or dark brown sugar

½ cup (1 stick) unsalted butter, softened

3 eggs

4 ounces unsweetened chocolate, melted and cooled

1 ½ teaspoons pure vanilla

1 cup dairy sour cream

1 cup very strong hot brewed coffee

Icing (your favorite)

DIRECTIONS:

Preheat oven to 350°F. Grease 2 9-inch square pans and line them with waxed paper; set aside. Sift together flour, baking soda, and salt; set aside. In a mixing bowl, combine brown sugar, butter, and eggs; beat with an electric mixer for 5 minutes or until mixture is very light and fluffy. Beat in chocolate and vanilla. Gradually add dry ingredients alternately with sour cream, beginning and ending with dry ingredients, and stirring just until blended after each addition. Add coffee and stir to mix. Pour batter into prepared pans. To release air bubbles in batter, hold cake pan 4 or 5 inches above countertop and then drop pan straight onto counter, being careful not to tip or spill the batter. Repeat with second cake pan. Bake at 350°F for 35 minutes. Remove from oven and place pans on a wire rack to cool for 15 minutes. Run a knife around the inside edges of each pan, then turn out cakes; remove waxed paper and cool cakes completely. Frost with your favorite icing.

Yields 12 to 16 servings

Recipe from The Michigan State University Experience, *courtesy of author Bob Bao*

RESOURCES

Before you head to the car, you may need to find the best place to get more information on throwing a great tailgate party, or where to find the stuff with which to do it. Of course, you'll find tailgating tips (including game-day and travel checklists), podcasts, videos, and recipes at both **theultimatetailgater.com** and **theultimatetailgatechef.com**, but there are also a number of other sources to help grow your tailgating knowledge.

You can find all sorts of helpful tools and information about tailgating from the **American Tailgaters Association** at atatailgate.com. The ATA is a national organization that promotes tailgating, offers members discounts on tailgating supplies and gear, reviews tailgating products, and more. I'm thrilled they endorse The Ultimate Tailgater books. Membership is free, and you can sign up online.

If you're looking for help getting tickets or finding a place to stay in any ACC city, **FanHub** can hook you up. They work with ticket brokers and hotel room wholesalers to find the best deals for traveling fans. They also have fan forums so you can learn more about the stadium and things to do in town, as well as pipe in with your own experiences and thoughts. You'll find it all at fanhub.com.

Of course, you'll also need tailgating gear if you want to do things like sit and eat. Don't worry, I'm here for you. From grills to frilly hats (be careful who you let see you wearing the frilly hat), there are thousands of resources online if you can't find anything in stores near you.

Grills and Accessories

Before buying it's a good idea to compare features and options to make sure you get the best grill for your style of tailgating. Some good sources of information and research are:

bbq.about.com/od/grills/index.htm?terms=grills

consumersearch.com/www/sports_and_leisure/gas-grill-reviews/index.html

With your new found grill knowledge, you're ready to get your grill. Here are some sites for tailgating grills and accessories:

bbqgalore.com
brinkmann.net
campchef.com
campingworld.com
ducane.com
freedomgrill.com
grillingaccessories.com
grilllovers.com
homedepot.com
lowes.com
webergrills.com

Tents

All across the Big Ten you'll find a sea of tents outside the stadium. For many tailgaters a canopy is enough. But for others, tents with sides and other options make for the ultimate tailgate party. You can find a variety of tents on these Web sites:

canopycenter.com
elitedeals.com/nctatelocate.html
eurekatents.com
ezupdirect.com
kdkanopy.com
shopping.com/xGS-Tailgating_Tents

General Tailgating Supplies

From licensed products, to coolers, to tables, to chairs, to . . . you get the idea.

americantailgater.com
collegegear.com
footballfanatics.com
tailgatehq.com
tailgatepartyshop.com
tailgatetown.com
tailgatingsupplies.com

Party Decorations

To turn your parking spot into a parking lot party, you need to dress it up. In addition to food, drinks, and friends, party lights, banners, and pom-poms help.

4funparties.com
bulkpartysupplies.com
party411.com
partyoptions.net/party_supply/football-main-page.htm
partypro.com
partyshelf.com/football.htm

Big Ten Schools and Teams

If you'd like to learn more about any of the 11 Big Ten schools and their athletic programs, you can visit these official sites. Many of the athletic sites also have links to additional statistics and news.

School Sites
Illinois: uiuc.edu
Indiana: indiana.edu
Iowa: uiowa.edu
Michigan: umich.edu
Michigan State: msu.edu
Minnesota: umn.edu
Northwestern: northwestern.edu

Ohio State:	osu.edu
Penn State:	psu.edu
Purdue:	purdue.edu
Wisconsin:	wisc.edu

Athletic Sites

Illinois:	fightingillini.cstv.com
Indiana:	iuhoosiers.cstv.com
Iowa:	hawkeyesports.cstv.com
Michigan:	mgoblue.com
Michigan State:	msuspartans.cstv.com
Minnesota:	gophersports.com
Northwestern:	nusports.cstv.com
Ohio State:	ohiostatebuckeyes.cstv.com
Penn State:	gopsusports.com
Purdue:	purduesports.cstv.com
Wisconsin:	uwbadgers.com

Alumni Association Sites

Illinois:	uiaa.org
Indiana:	alumni.indiana.edu
Iowa:	iowalum.com
Michigan:	alumni.umich.edu
Michigan State:	msualum.com
Minnesota:	alumni.umn.edu
Northwestern:	alumni.northwestern.edu
Ohio State:	ohiostatealumni.org
Penn State:	alumni.psu.edu
Purdue:	purduealum.org
Wisconsin:	uwalumni.com